2020 B..._ _ _

For more information, please contact:

Civin Media Relations,

2 Robbins Rd, Winchendon, MA 01475

978-502-1453

ISBN-13: 9798574053621

Imprint Civin Media Relations

<u>Dedication</u>

I'm so grateful to have so many kind people in my life who have helped create so many memories. There are so many more blessings I have shared in this book entitled Blessed with Memories.

Thank you to friends and family.

~ Bill ~

Foreword

What a privilege it is to write this intro to Bill Pennington's book! Bill has been an inspiration to me for many years and for many reasons. The stories he shares in this enjoyable work attest to his penchant for not only recognizing qualities in others – but celebrating them.

Starting with the respect, admiration and love he has for his parents and family members who have served our country, the value Bill places on those who have made such sacrifice is paramount in his life – value he doesn't just hold personally, but that he lives by every day. It is the basis for the now iconic Run for the Troops in Andover, MA – conceived and brought to fruition by Bill to support military veterans, and in a few short years becoming one of the area's most successful fundraisers.

It isn't the name, the game, or the season, that have brought people on board. It is Bill's contagious can-do spirit and his sincere desire to help that spearheaded a whole community to come together in support of this important cause. He is a person of modest means and words. But he uses both well to make things happen - quietly sharing stories that move us, such as the veteran who lost his legs in combat, and has three kids to raise, or the military spouse who not only lost her husband, but also her son to suicide following tours overseas. We all hear them. But Bill answers a personal inner call help them. And somehow, he finds a way.

Thus this book! Several years ago Bill came to Ironstone Farm and heard our story…of when we saw our horses positively impact the lives of veterans suffering with Post Traumatic Stress and launched the Equine Encounter program, opening the door for vets to experience the mysteries of the horse/human relationship. We share the concept of "the longer they stay, the more effective the long-term success". And their families, and their loved ones left behind when so many of our veterans lose their battle with anxiety and depression – all can be helped through this unique connection.

Ironstone Farm is changing their lives – and, as Bill keeps saying - we can do so much more! In this spirit, we are renovating the original farmhouse at Ironstone to become a retreat center for veterans, first responders, and their families. The project is 100% dependent on contributed dollars – the typical non-profit mantra of "raise a little, build a little"! The house is a labor of love – much of it built by volunteer hands with funds raised through volunteer efforts. Once complete, it will become a center for healing and joy - for those people who captured Bill's heart long ago, who have protected and sacrificed for us since our country was founded, and who deserve to find the peace that the natural surroundings of Ironstone Farm and its animals can give them.

So read the stories, be inspired, and know that in so doing you are helping a dream come true. For Bill, as he is doggedly determined to help us finish this project and get those doors opened; for all the volunteers who have worked so hard because they believe in the difference this special place will make; but mostly for the people who will use it - who come to us, stay awhile, and leave healed, happy and ready to move on with their lives.

Deedee O'Brien
Co-Founder and Executive Director Emeritus
Challenge Unlimited at Ironstone Farm

Chapter 1
Friends I Never Met

RAGBRAI

I've spent a good chunk of my life on two wheels. In fact, I have spent a total of more than 20 weeks over the course of two decades, trekking across the glorious state of Iowa. Alongside thousands of other cyclists, I have pedaled an average of 450 miles as part of "RAGBRAI," the Des Moines Register's Annual Great Bicycle Ride Across Iowa. Established in 1973, the annual event has attracted riders from all over the world. More than 320,000 people have pedaled RAGBAI since the inception of the event. Each year, the course shifts to a new area of the state and has been held in all 99 counties of Iowa.

What started out as a "dad's vacation" for this stay-at-home father from Andover, Massachusetts, has turned into a celebration of life that has allowed me to connect with "friends he's never met," year after year. Over time, I've amassed quite a few memories and here are a few of my favorites:

Chicken Rodeo

Riding into Vining, Iowa, during my 10th cycle of RAGBRAI on a Sunday morning, I decided to attend an 8:30 a.m. service at Vining Alliance Church. I often like to attend church services when I'm visiting the Midwest. Following the service, the church hosted a chicken barbecue. But it was a chicken barbecue unlike anything I had ever been to before.

Outside of the church was a 30-foot by 30-foot pen with roughly 20 chickens scurrying around inside. After inquiring about the meal, I was promptly handed a rope, instructed to catch a chicken and hand it over to the butcher once I'd retrieved it. While not exactly a common occurrence in my world, I can't say I was really surprised by the activity held in the town that had a population of 50 in 2010.

Lassoing the fowl wasn't that difficult, even as foreign as the task might have been. Although, to this day, I'm still unsure if the chicken I captured was actually the one I dined on, I do remember one thing: it tasted great.

Showered with hospitality

RAGBRAI is held every year during the last week of July, when average high temperatures in Iowa consistently hit the mid-80s. As you can imagine, pedaling an average of 60 miles each day in the heat, showers are a premium. They tend to be really hard to find when you're staying at campgrounds and most tend to be cold water. Some places even hook up showers at car washes.

During one of my rides into Dyersville, I pulled up to this Victorian-style, six-bedroom home on Main Street along the route that had a lemonade stand out front. While partaking in some deliciously refreshing lemonade, I struck up a conversation with the owners of the home and shortly thereafter, they offered up the shower in their home to me. "Make yourself at home," they told me. The timing was actually perfect as I was headed over to the Field of Dreams baseball field, which was originally built for the 1989 movie bearing the same name, to buy a change of clothes - a T-shirt and a pair of shorts.

After purchasing the clothes, I returned and was led into the historic home for a nice hot shower. The owners didn't think anything of it.

If I was flexible enough, I think I would have done a cartwheel.

Tymes Remembered Tea Room in T-shirts

It was around the 1997 RAGBAI that I dined with my sister's team, Team McDuck, at one of the best restaurants in Central Iowa in our T-shirts. Tymes Remembered Tea Room in Perry, Iowa, was an upscale restaurant that featured many porcelain figurines along the walls. The restaurant, housed in a building that was constructed in 1920, was a significant tourist attraction, but held a high-end casual dress code. You could see ladies in cocktail dresses and men dressed well, though not necessarily in suit and tie. I felt like a bull in a china shop dressed in my T-shirt and true to form almost knocked down a figurine.

When the server handed out laminated menus that were marked with lower prices than normal, I was a little surprised. "Is the food that bad?" I asked with a laugh. The server told us that the establishment didn't feel like it was fair to charge its customers full price when the "normal standard" of service couldn't be provided. I was stunned. The place was packed to the gills and they knew it was going to be with the thousands of cyclists from RAGBRAI. If this was Cape Cod, business owners would have instead jacked up the prices.

Greg, Bill, Melissa and Nancy

We were extremely pleased with the service. I think I had pulled pork or barbecue and probably three slices of apple pie. We left our server a tremendous tip.

A flat tire and a friendly gesture

Holly Dargie, a friend of mine from Andover, joined me on a ride around 2001. On the first day, Holly stopped me to tell me that something was wrong with her bike. She hit something on the course and ended up with a flat tire. I told her not to worry as most attractive women don't have to worry when there's an issue with their bicycle. I advised her that she might want to turn her bike upside down, reach down and untie her shoes. I told her I'd stand on the opposite side of the road to observe and not hinder her.

"When you stand back up, someone will offer to change your tire," I assured her.

And wouldn't you know, that's exactly what happened. A gentleman came over to help her and she stood there the whole time smiling as he changed the tire.

Two days later, I ended up with a flat tire myself. Holly offered to stand on the opposite side of the road while I waited for help just as I had. I told her that I probably wouldn't be as lucky. And I wasn't.

I ended up changing the tire myself. You see, there's probably a 60/40 male-to-female ratio there. Holly just laughed.

Mark and Bill wander through the corn field

In the days before GPS, my friend Mark Lussier and I followed a road map straight into a dead end. Mark kept saying, "I'm pretty sure this road will intersect soon." But it didn't.

Ultimately, he suggested we take a short cut through a cornfield because "the road has to be on the other side of it." We ended up biking about 70 miles in 95-degree weather. When we finally hit the road on the

9

other side, we were met by a Trooper from the Iowa State Patrol who asked what we were doing coming out of the corn field.

After telling him what had happened, he indicated that the road had been plowed under about five years ago but had apparently never been changed on maps.

Understanding that we needed to stop to get water and rest a bit, we decided to visit a farmhouse we'd spotted half-a-mile up the road. We had about ten miles left to go before we made it to our campsite, so if we grabbed some water, I knew we'd be fine.

When we got to the house, I knocked at the door and was greeted by a woman. I told her that we were just ten miles away from our campsite and were hoping to ask if we could use her hose to cool down and grab some water.

"Absolutely not," she said. "You guys can come on inside."

But that wasn't all.

She further proceeded to invite us in to freshen up, have supper and even stay the night. This was around the mid-1990s, before cell phones were a thing. Her husband hadn't even arrived home yet, and here she was inviting us to stay for the night. But even after he came home, we all chatted like we had been friends for 50 years.

The next morning, the homeowners, Mary and John, served us a breakfast of pancakes and bacon with loads of orange juice like it was nothing special. I don't think we even caught their last names. They just offered up hugs after breakfast and sent us on our way.

A tornado and a bank vault

At around 10:30 p.m. in 1999, I was having cocktails with a group at an outside bar in Le Mars, Iowa, when tornado sirens sounded.

Our campground was probably five to six miles away and was assuredly not the safest place to be. We decided to look for the oldest building in the downtown as a safe bet. If it's been around that long, we'll probably be safe, we figured.

We started walking around the downtown and ran into this woman that must have been in her 80's and asked her where she suggested we go.

"Go to the vault," she said, motioning over to the bank.

So we headed over to the unofficial storm shelter and bounded down the stairs to something that resembled a Budweiser commercial. There were around 35 people down there with everything you can imagine - all kinds of food and kegs of beer - that was rolled out of the vault. Everyone was relaxing and a sound system was playing tunes. We hung out until around 2:30 a.m.

Bill at RAGBRAI 2018 just before losing his cell phone.

Luckily, we made a friend that had a pick-up truck that brought us back to the campground around 3:30 a.m. People were getting up early to ride and assess if there had been any damage that resulted from the tornado. Fortunately, there was no damage to our site. We were in our late 20's at this stage, so we decided just to pack things up and hit the road. We rode out 30 to 35 miles and took a nap until the early afternoon.

A tornado helmet

Kenny Shapiro and I have been friends for a long time - about 30 years. We have a bit of an unusual friendship. He can be a bit stubborn.

Oftentimes, if I recommend that he do something, he won't do it only because I recommended it.

Either way, Kenny was a very experienced RAGBRAI participant. His tent was near mine and Lori Becker's when the tornado sirens went off at around 9:30 p.m. in 2002. The shelter was about 50 to 60 feet away. Laurie and I get up and I yelled to Kenny to do the same. At the time, Kenny had set up his tent under a fairly large-sized tree.

"I don't know," Kenny says. "Maybe in I'll come."

But Kenny never came in.

As it turns out, someone died in the storm and a tree did fall about a half a mile away from where we were. I bumped into Kenny the next morning and told him. And he said, "Bill, I just put on my helmet and brought my bike in. And that's the end of that."

He's one of the smartest guys I know. But even when he was wrong, he was right.

Lost, but quickly found

One year, I was on about mile 30 of the 75-mile day, and I remember stopping on Main Street in Burlington and reaching for my cell phone only to find that it wasn't there. These days, I always carry my cell phone as I have some health issues. I was wearing a bike jersey that had pockets in the back. I remember putting it in my back middle pocket, but as it turns out, there was a hole there.

In a very Easterner-like way, I voiced that I was very upset that I couldn't find my cell phone.

When I asked a man named Jim at an information booth, he just replied, it "happens all the time."

"Relax, this is Iowa. By the time you go to the overnight town, someone will return it," he said. "We guarantee it."

When I pulled into the information center in the overnight town, which is where I was directed to go, I saw two women talking and one had my phone in her hand. I had a couple of cards tucked into the back of the case and was able to verify that it was mine.

My cell phone wasn't the only thing that was lost that day. In fact, later on, we went to a concert down by the water where there were more than 2,000 people in the parking lot. Alan Carroll was in charge of the van and when I asked about getting back to the van, Alan said he didn't know where the keys were.

"They must be around here somewhere," he said.

We started talking to the police to see if an announcement could be made. About ten minutes later we headed to the stage where the bands were playing to see if we could speak to the person in charge to make an announcement about the missing keys. As soon as we got there, before even talking to anyone, the band stopped playing.

"We have an announcement," a band member stated. "A pair of keys have been found."

Those missing keys were ours. Two items lost in one day and both were found right away.

"Only in Iowa," I said.

Biker Down

I'm on blood thinners. About five years ago, I had a heart attack. My blood doesn't clot very well because of the blood thinners, so the worst thing I could do is crash. But last year, one of the biggest highlights was what occurred when I did crash.

The five people I was riding with were extremely good friends of mine. We were all getting on our bikes and leaving. My friends were about 150 yards away. I made some forward movement on my bike - I wasn't going fast at all - and this big crack in the road caused me to fall over. Whenever someone falls, everyone yells, "Biker down!" But as soon as I fell, my friends ran as fast as they could to see if I was alright.

They dropped their bikes without looking back. They're all in great shape, but not exactly spring chickens. It might seem like a simple thing, but to have people jump into action like that, was definitely a memorable moment.

I walked away with scrapes and my fingers scratched and I definitely got teased about it for the rest of the week, but it was without a doubt one of my favorite moments of 2019.

I knew they were good friends of mine, but people often talk a good game, and to see them fly into action, knowing they truly care - see them come through - was such a huge thing.

Melissa lands in a tornado

Five years ago, around May 7, I had a heart attack. Obviously, I survived and had a couple of stents put in. My son, Greg, daughter, Melissa and sister, Nancy, had been planning to join me in Iowa for well over a year when the heart attack happened. Melissa was very nervous about her dad doing RAGBRAI as it was taking place only twelve weeks after I had a heart attack. I was still planning on doing RAGBRAI, and now, I was more motivated than ever.

Melissa, who was 23 at the time, was flying into Council Bluffs Municipal Airport on a Friday in 2015. I had the van with me and we were doing the ride out, on the last day of the ride. I've always had a really good idea of the weather, and Melissa, being my daughter, also had a keen sense of the weather. Because of that, we'd often talk about the forecast. She told me she had been watching the radar, and noticed that it was a very deep red, and because tornadoes most often go from west to east, she was very concerned.

I was approaching the airport and watching the storms, which were 60 to 70 miles away. Council Bluffs was a very small airport and as she came through the gate, tornado sirens began to sound.

"C'mon Miss, we've got to go," I said to her, noting that the storms were about 50 miles to the west. "We have to move."

I threw her stuff in the back and we headed out. Melissa was checking the radar from her phone. We were going as fast as we could, but Melissa reiterated that we needed to be moving even faster.

"See that lightning flash up there, one is to the north and south," she said.

"I understand, Miss," I said. "But we're in the middle of Iowa, where are we going to go?"

"Is there an overpass?" she asked.

The moment was reminiscent of the 1996 action movie, "Twister." I wasn't sure we were going to make it. But like I told Melissa, "they made it in Twister, so we're going to make it, too."

She told me to pull over, but I kept driving.

There was hay flying through the air.

I'm not sure if it was the craziest or stupidest thing I've ever done, but we made it to Atlantic, Iowa, safe and sound.

Team McDucks

My sister, Nancy "Duck" Pennington, is a physical education teacher and very much into team-building.

She got the nickname Duck Butt because her butt would stick up in the air as a child. They shortened it to "Duck" - We called her Mother Duck.

The 25th anniversary of RAGBRAI was about 22 years ago. For the celebration, we wanted to have 25 Team McDuck members. We ended up with riders that were either from states that began with an "M" or a "C," including Minnesota, Massachusetts, California or Connecticut, thus named the team accordingly.

My sister was into making people "earn their wings." Team members wore Scottish-style theme hats that had basically shoelaces to keep their hat on.

"You had to earn your wings," she'd say.

She was like the "Mother Duck" and required that team members had to set up her tent and all the veteran tents, so that they'd earn points along the way. If some of the rookies were ahead of us, they'd put stickers on, and put "Team McDuck approved" and if some rookie would do that, they'd earn their wings. We had duck calls. We were very easy to spot and were able to meet as a group over at Joe's Bar & Grill.

It was a Friday night. The ceremony was held every year and we'd all give a little talk about how each person earned their wings. I would design the costumes and my sister would organize the event. We'd get together every once in a while, through phone calls or cards.

Sister Mary

I was so excited. I couldn't go to RAGBRAI the first year, but I was here now. It was 1991. I was supposed to be in the designated campground around 3 o'clock. I was supposed to be riding with the Des Moines Cycle Club. I flew into Council Bluffs Municipal Airport and I met this extremely attractive blonde wearing an Iowa T-shirt, who was also headed to RAGBRAI.

"Where do we go now?" I asked her.

We ended up being tourists and I arrived late.

I set up my tent 500 to 600 yards away from the Des Moines Cycle Club, where there were 250 people with them. After I set it up, Mary and I decided to look for my sister Nancy.

Mary was dressed to the hilt. She wore pearls and a dress. I was married at the time and so was Mary. She was a financial planner from Philadelphia. We didn't do anything that would ever get us into trouble, but we did become extremely close for a while.

I introduced her as my sister to everyone: "This is Sister Mary."

She was part of my first experience from RAGBRAI and we went to Dyersville together.

Coming up over the hill into Dyersville was just like a moment out of the movie "Field of Dreams." We were going to my favorite place in the world and I was biking alongside someone I've had so much fun with. Mary and I remained good friends for a long time before we eventually lost touch.

A little advice to my friends

I had ridden into Ankeny, Iowa, when I spotted a tremendous refreshment stand. People were zooming on by and I decided to slow down. The stand was raising money for the Ankeny High School little league cheerleaders.

"Can I help you here?" I asked.

After they agreed, I suggested moving the cheerleaders out in the streets with signs. The barricades will make the riders slow down. I further directed them to put the apple pies and Gatorades they were selling up front.

Before you knew it, riders started to slow down and stop by. The stand sold out within two hours.

"What can we ever do for you?" the group asked.

All I requested was a letter to my home in Massachusetts. And they did. It was great feeling knowing that I could help like that. I still have the letter as a memory of the experience.

Bill Does Iowa
By Ken Shapiro

Words that come to mind immediately when I describe Bill include biking, running, Iowa, outgoing, people person, adventurous, and doing right by his family and friends.

Bill was a part of our original biking group. In the early days, we would begin our rides between 6:30 a.m. - 7:00 a.m. We would ask around to members of the group, "What time do you have to be back?" This way, we could judge when the group should plan on returning to Andover. Almost always, Bill would respond that he definitely had to be back by 9:00 a.m. The return times of the other riders were more flexible than Bill's.

Towards the tail end of our rides, we would circle back to "drop off" Bill at his house. To be safe or because the group was riding fast, we would often find ourselves nearing Bill's house between 8:30-8:45. Instead of going immediately home, he would say "let's keep riding.". At first, we didn't understand. We knew he had to be home in order to go to church with his family but we soon came to realize was that Bill wanted to squeeze every minute of "Bill time" out of his morning, while at the same time, probably looking to incur less "ball and chain" time.

The RAGBRAI is an annual fun-filled seven day bike ride that goes across the state of Iowa. When I first met up with Bill on "The Ride", he had brought a small group of family and friends that he was introducing to the experience. Bill, their esteemed leader, brought them to Iowa as a group he affectionately referred to as Team McDuck. He got them all matching outfits, including shirts and hats, rubber ducks for their bikes, all "duck" themed accompaniments and they made nicknames for each of themselves - Bill Duck, Mother Duck, Quackers, Ducky, etc. They rode together, camped together, and generally did everything together. I personally found it a bit annoying, but sai la vie. He asked me numerous times to join his little merry band, but I would have nothing to do with them, and I politely refused. I think that he eventually understood my reluctance, especially since he never repeated bringing a themed group to the ride again.

One year, Bill felt that he wanted more than just the seven days of fun and decided to extend the ride - basically adding an additional 250 miles pre-ride. Bill has the ability to talk people into doing things. He persuaded his friend Mark not only into doing the RAGBRAI for the first time, but also into doing the extra 250 mile ride out with him. Mark had never camped before, let alone ridden that large number of consecutive *miles. Needless-to-say, Bill provided both of them with quite an adventure.*

Mark, while a brilliant tech guy, was fairly clueless, and didn't have a lick of common sense, or worldliness, about him. Well, that afternoon, after the rest of us showed up in our nice air conditioned buses to the start of the official ride, Mark and Bill dragged in. They were hot, sweaty, and looked rough. They looked like a couple of tired pups after three days together on the road. While Mark went off to retrieve all of his brand new camping gear that he recently purchased as he had owned nothing pre-ride, Bill was just shaking his head, bitching, moaning and telling tales of how painful it was to ride with Mark due to his naivety and all his wackiness. He then had to go off, and teach Mark how to set up his tent, where to clean up, how to forage for food, etc. Bill did not neglect his responsibilities, so for the rest of the trip, he had to be Mark's 24/7 babysitter, guiding him and trying to keep him out of trouble. Years later, when Bill's bike died, Bill talked Mark into buying him a brand new $5000 bike. Bill's fellow riders figured that it was either payback for Bill taking such good care of Mark at that time, or it was just Bill's strength of persuasiveness.

Oh and by the way, the RAGBRAI pre-ride out that Bill began in our circle of riders, has carried on over the years. It turned out to be just as much fun as the actual ride. We've stayed at hole in the wall places like The Dew Drop Inn, camped at the famous Albert The Bull statue, and found many other interesting places. We've played bingo in town centers, cooled off in local swimming pools, jumped into passing rivers, and bowled in towns while waiting for passing rains to subside. And that's all thanks to Bill.

Bill loves the state of Iowa. He worships at the church of the Field of Dreams in Dyersville. He always inquires about real estate costs, local cost of living, and hopes to someday settle there.

There is no chair that Bill will not sit in, and "chat for a spell". He will sit down with just about anyone and begin conversing. Interacting with young and old is his M.O. (method of operation). Often, we'd hit a small ride-thru town, and Bill will just start talking with the local folk - seniors, church folk, kids, firemen, policemen, store owners, etc. Anybody and everybody. He asks about crop outputs, or the local hero, how the town got its name, or "how many hogs can you fit in one of those trailers?" He never lacks for conversation when it comes to talking with the Iowa locals, and is totally in his element when doing so.

Many people along the way who are selling things are not the best marketers. Bill loves to help organizations sell more stuff. Once we were riding rapidly down a hill and there was a farm family selling watermelon slices benefitting their local church. Nobody was stopping due to the awkward hillside location and the full table of watermelon slices not being sold was a sad sight to Bill. The family and their kids were quite disappointed at how things were going. Everyone was just flying, and not realizing what a great treat they were missing, and at a good price. We stopped and Bill showed the family kids how to stand up the road a few hundred feet uphill, before their driveway, holding the slices up in the air, and told them what to say to the riders going past. He got out there with them and showed them exactly how to do it. He generated excitement in those shy kids, with the positive attitude of making the sales. It only took a few minutes, and riders started pulling off the road. When we left 25 minutes later, the place was packed, and they were successfully selling watermelon slices like hotcakes!

Each town on the Iowa ride has a festival type atmosphere and there are all kinds of things going on. There are musical groups, umpah bands, singing groups (like the Singing Elvis's), baton twirlers, gymnastic groups, etc. There are antique tractors being shown and vintage cars lined up. Some towns use a strung up beer keg on an overhead wire that opposing firetruck water hoses use to try to push to the keg to the opposition's side (like a tug of war). Every town has something interesting to experience. We stopped in one town, and Bill said to me, "Have I got a treat for you! Follow me."

The next thing I know, I am being challenged to a very unique competition - a toilet bowl race. I am at a starting line, sitting atop a toilet, mounted on a wood board base with wheels with a toilet plunger in my hands to use like a canoe paddle. Soon I am going down a hill, with riders cheering me on, racing against Bill to the finish line - albeit fairly slowly, and not in a straight line. And just as I feel the proximity of victory, I am thwarted by Bill using his plunger to push me sideways. His dirty play threw a wrench into my forward motion, and a planned first place finish. While trying to get my forward momentum going again, he easily shot himself over the finish line! That stinker! We couldn't stop laughing!

On RAGBRAI, there are KYBOs. This is what the temporary port-a-potty toilets are affectionately referred to on The Ride. Kybo is a funny acronym that stands for "keep your bowels open!" While Bill was not responsible for first imparting that important terminology to me, he did teach me about the betting game, Kybo Roulette. One day, we stopped in a pass-thru town, and there was a line of kybos with a line of riders waiting to use them. He found a marker, some paper and a roll of tape. He marked 1-5 on each of the paper sheets, and then taped each of them on the outside kybo doors. Next thing I know he's shouting for bets, and *quickly taking $1 bets from each of five bettors. The rider that successfully calls the first kybo door to open, wins the accumulated funds!*

One day, we stopped to have some lunch. We were sitting on a convenient sidewalk curb. Next thing we knew, we heard what sounded like snoring. We turned around looking for the source, and saw Bill on his back, on the sidewalk, snoring away with not a care in the world! It turned out that it wasn't a rare occurrence, as Bill loves laying down and napping – often times directly on the concrete sidewalks.

Bill is what we call a strong, steady rider. One RAGBRAI day, Bill and I were gently riding across the Iowa landscape of corn and soybeans. When I say gently riding, I mean we weren't riding with a group of riders, putting the pedal to the metal, as we often want to do. We were just moving along, side by side, cruising at a slower than usual pace - maybe 10-11 mph - just chatting up a storm. Not really paying attention, we passed many slower riders. After a period of time, Bill says, "Don't turn around now, but I believe that we have a few riders, that are drafting us". We almost never rode this slowly, and I didn't think we could be going fast enough for anyone to benefit getting air, from drafting off of us, so I couldn't believe what he was saying. Sure enough, after a bit, I did take a look, and it turned out that there was a dual liner of riders behind us. And there were a lot of them - we counted almost 50 riders once we pulled off the line!

As I mentioned earlier, Bill talks people into things. He's like Tom Sawyer getting his fence painted by others. Eight years ago, he talked me into presenting the food at his start up fund raising road run - The Run For The Troops. That year there were only 150 participants, and a dozen volunteers. I've been helping out ever since. As the years have gone by, The Run has grown exponentially, now with thousands of participants, and a full team of volunteers that Bill has pressed into service. Bill's volunteers have been loyal, and they appreciate what he puts together. Bill has proven to be a doer, and a strong passionate motivator. I always marvel at Bill's ability to believe in himself and others, and how he makes things happen.

I look forward to many years of experiences with Bill.

A Class Act
Ben Kellman

There was one guy at kindergarten parents' night wearing a Boston Marathon jacket. Just like mine. And that is where this starts in about 1995-96. We were soon biking together, somewhat irregularly. He introduced me to some of his riding pals, all faster than me, as well as some running pals, all faster than me again. But when we rode in a group, this guy, who was arguably stronger and faster than everyone else in the group, would ride with me. I could end this little tale about Bill Pennington right here, because that comment is enough information on who he is. He would slow down his ride, make sure that I was okay, and maybe encourage me to go a little beyond what I could do and let me make the ride mine. A class act.

But there is more.

He convinced me to go with him, and 10,000 of his closest friends, to bicycle across Iowa, the year I turned 50. Camp for grownups! And over the years, there were countless rides where somewhere during the course of two to five hours of riding, we would stop talking to each other, fuming. We have different political views and know for certain that the other guy's brain just doesn't work right, sometimes showing his ignorance and naivete. Also Bill just likes to rile you up sometimes for fun. Did I already mention many miles of not speaking? And yet, we often found middle ground, solving a big issue, and thought we should become co-Presidents together. There were many things we talked about and didn't act on. But some deep life changing episodes were shared and partially resolved on many of those rides.

One last thing, about Bill's generosity. I'm sure folks know how he has acted in many ways to make the world a better place by organizing fun fund raisers. Maybe you don't know that Bill has a big bucket, where he daily drops his change and some of his poker winnings. Just before the first weekend in August, he brings these hundreds of dollars to my house, supporting my Pan Mass Challenge ride. Generosity is in his blood.

Run, walk, sit or ride with him, and you are suddenly with a friend.

Chapter 2
26.2 x 53 = Many Miles of My Marathons

I've run 53 marathons, including my favorite of them all, the Boston Marathon 21 times. The first one I ever ran was in 1978 in Newport, Rhode Island where I finished in a respectable first marathon time of 3:17:00 minutes. I started doing marathons due to a silly fraternity dare when I wanted to do something crazy physically. I trained for only six months for that race.

My fastest time ever was a pretty respectable 2:38:00 in Duluth, Minnesota in 1986. This was an average of six minutes a mile, which is not elite speed, but pretty darn fast.

The following year after the Newport Marathon, I got into it more. In order to qualify for the Boston Marathon for the men's 40-49 category, I needed to average 6 minutes and 45 seconds per mile or a 2:49:41 marathon time.

In 1980, I ran a close, but no cigar time of 2:56:00. In 1981, I ran a marathon in East Lyme Connecticut. I was recording each and every mile to ensure I hit my goal. My plan was to run each mile at a 6:30 pace to ultimately reach my goal. With every passing mile, I was feeling pretty confident. That is, until I reached mile 25. Suddenly I realized that I didn't calculate for the last 2/10ths of the 26.2 marathon distance.

In the end, I missed the qualifying time by 52 seconds and again no cigar.

Six weeks later in Newport, Rhode Island, I calculated my pace to finish at least one minute under my goal time. When I hit mile 24, I said to myself: "I got this."

Then, I made the turn onto Wellington Avenue. It was right on the water, the wind was severe and blew right in my face. I managed to tuck inside some people that were running behind me. I was so worried that I may not be able to make it yet again, but I did - by 11 seconds; finishing in 02:49:30.

I qualified for the Boston Marathon, which was a big goal of mine. At the time, it was one of the few marathons that you had to qualify for in order to participate, so this was pretty big for me.

A scene from Bill's favorite movie, Field of Dreams.

Bill

Melissa and Dad and a Forever Memory

Bill and Kevin Dykstra after a long ride on the road.

Iowa 2019 Team Ride Out drinking some Ruthie's Beer at Cumming's Tap Cummings, Iowa—Population 407

Bill, Nancy and Melissa at wondering who's in charge at RAGBRAI 2015

The Ride Out group at Knucklehead's Bar– RAGBRAI 2015

Why don't you win?

There were four words that ignited another level of motivation and they came from the lips of my father. While he had no idea what he was saying and meant no harm, he asked me one day: "Why don't you win?"

He was just curious.

"Ya know what Dad? I'm going to find out," I told him.

So, I got myself tested to find out just why I couldn't win.

My dad had very big legs and was nearly 6 feet tall. My mother was 5 foot 11 inches. The most elite runners are typically small and chicken-boned. I wasn't and certainly am not.

I went to a lab where they studied athletic performance via an Oxygen Uptake test. I had a connection that allowed me to get in. They put a mask over my face and put tubes in to measure how much CO_2 you had in you and how much oxygen you can take in. They took muscle fibers from my legs to see if my muscles were suited for long-distance running. My genetics were not helping me there. I needed slow-twitch muscles for endurance. I made a better sprinter than a marathon runner.

My body fat was only six percent, so I couldn't lose any more weight.

Doctors told me my oxygen uptake was phenomenal, that I had a Cadillac engine in a Cadillac. The best runners in the world have Cadillac engines in a Volkswagen.

So, I went back and told my dad: "If I didn't have your big legs or mom's big bone structure, I probably could win."

Not running straight East Lyme 1982

I was trying to focus on achieving a time of 2:38:00. I was running in East Lyme, Connecticut, with my best friend at the time, Mark Lussier. It was a humid day, but only about 60 degrees. Mark and I were running together, I get to mile 10 and it was becoming a big effort. I couldn't understand it. I was running 6-minute miles. That time is good, but it shouldn't be this hard. Then we got to mile 15. Mark says, "Bill, I don't feel well."

We get to mile 18, where my sister was riding along the side of the course on her bike. She notes that I haven't run a straight line in over a mile. She told me that I kept weaving. I told her I didn't know why and asked her for a Coke. Nancy always supported me and always had extra fluids on hand.

By mile 24, I started to feel better, but then it got warm again. It was about 85 degrees out and I was actually shivering. I started to have problems again with only one mile left to go.

I was having some real difficulties. I couldn't even stand up. I did finish but immediately had medical personnel lead me into the medical tent. They took my temperature and I was basically out of it. They told me I was dehydrated and needed some fluids quickly. What I realized that day though was that if this was the worst thing that will happen, it eliminated all fear. From that point onward, I realized that I could still finish and I don't have to be scared about anything. If the worst thing is that I end up in the medical tent and they give me fluids, then I'll be okay in anything I attempt from that point forward.

Running with Scott

My Uncle Scott sent me a letter when I told him about my desire to share my marathon stories in a book.

Bill,

Joyce told me you wanted some of my thoughts on the marathon for your book. I thought you were joking about writing a book, but it looks like you are serious, which is neat. Best of luck!

Here is my input: In 1980, the U.S. Army assigned me to a three year tour at my alma mater, the University of Rhode Island, to serve as an ROTC instructor. Joyce and I were thrilled since we would be around both of our families for a while. For the first time in some years, I had a fairly regular and not overwhelming schedule.

I had always enjoyed running and the Army emphasized physical fitness, Since I had the time, I started to increase my mileage. With encouragement from my brother-in-law, Bill Pennington, I began to participate in road races.

Shortly after the 1982 Blessing of the Fleet Road Race, Bill made me an offer. He would get me entered in the Boston Marathon, which he ran regularly and would coach me if I agreed to stop smoking.

Coach Bill set up my training calendar, which included specific mileage as well as hill training. He even accompanied me on the long 20 mile run. He constantly stayed in touch with me to offer encouragement and advice.

On a chilly April morning in 1983, we traveled together to Boston. After a bus ride to the start line at Hopkinton we wore large black garbage bags until the gun went off.

Bill, an experienced long distance runner, could have taken off like a rocket, but he chose to stay with me, setting a pace he knew would ensure my success. He was right about Wellesley; that was a crazy, fun-loving crowd. The run went pretty well although Bill again was correct about the challenge of Heartbreak Hill. My legs really started to feel it, but Bill's motivating comments and spirit got me through the final six miles.

I will never forget crossing the finish line. I felt an immense sense of pride and accomplishment when I received my finisher's medallion, which I still have. I also have the framed picture of us crossing together at 03:19:30. It's in front of me as I type these thoughts.

I owe it all to Bill.

Sincerely, Uncle Scott

KC Marathon

The Kansas City Marathon took place in 1985 and was a relatively small marathon with only about 500 to 600 runners. I was running with Health Plus, a health club focused on runners.

At the time, I was training with a good friend of mine, Tom Dowling. During the weekend, I was getting 26-32 miles in totaling about 100 miles a week. I thought I could come close to winning but didn't think I could quite pull it off.

My girlfriend, Brooke who would later become my wife, rode alongside the course, and said, "Bill, they're just ahead of you."

I ended up finishing in third place which was really an accomplishment. United Airlines sponsored the marathon, so I imagined the prizes would be great. The first place winner ran the marathon in 2 hours and 34 minutes and was awarded airline tickets anywhere in the world for two people. *Bingo! I should get some tickets too!*

The second place winner ran the marathon in 2 hours and 38 minutes was awarded two tickets for anywhere in the U.S.

And third place! I ran the marathon in 2 hours and 40 minutes. Well, third place was…a nice coffee mug. A. Coffee. Mug. How do we go from a gold medal winning prize of a trip anywhere in the world and silver, anywhere in the U.S. to bronze with a coffee mug?

32 miles a week

In 1986, my then wife Brooke and I moved to Stone Mountain, Georgia and I continued to train hard. I got a heart rate monitor and hooked up with a nutritionist because I was working outside at a physical job and was consuming 4,000 to 5,000 calories a day.

I was consuming a high carb energy drink regularly that was also extremely high in sugar, but I was burning a lot of calories.

I had been training along Stone Mountain where mile 16 to 22 was pretty hilly. I was confident I could do well at the Boston Marathon with a steady diet of Stone Mountain training.

I arrived four days ahead of time to run Boston. Typically, you don't run as much right before marathon day as you taper down in distance, but I did and I kept consuming this high-carb, high-energy drink.

When I hit mile 16 in Boston, I started cramping up because there was so much sugar in my body. I had run 26 to 32 miles every Sunday, but I couldn't understand why I was cramping up. As it turns out, I was basically dehydrated.

I still finished, but in a pretty unspectacular time and I could not walk afterwards.

I knew I was in great shape but couldn't understand what I had done wrong. I don't know who was more upset at the time, Brooke or me. I worked hard following the race to get healthy again.

Grandma's Marathon

About seven weeks later, in the middle of June of 1986, I flew up to Duluth, Minnesota to participate in Grandma's Marathon. It was a near religious experience to those who participated.

The weather in Minneapolis and St. Paul, Minnesota was between 80 and 90 degrees and 80 to 90 percent humidity. The weather in Duluth, however, was 45 degrees with low humidity.

My plan at that point was to drink nothing but water. I was confident I could do this and was praying a lot.

"God, just give me one chance," I prayed. "This has to be the time."

I was running with a group of guys at a pace of about 6-minute mile, with the intention of finally breaking 2 hours and 40 minutes.

I was paying close attention to my split times and noticed by mile 21 that not only was I keeping pace, but it seemed as though I'd gotten faster.

"God, this is in your hands," I prayed.

For the last four miles, I felt like I was running on a cloud. It was so easy.

I reached mile 25 and the last mile was on cobblestones. I maneuvered that last bumpy stretch and I was the first finisher in my age group with a time of 2:38:00. I actually ran back and got my friends after I finished, which means I probably totaled more than 30 miles that day.

Sometimes the fastest runs are the easiest.

I had trained so hard for that event and I still get emotional talking about it. I had run 15 marathons prior at around 2 hours and 40 minutes. I was 31 years old. My wife and all of my friends were so supportive, telling me they wanted me to do my best.

It was like my Olympic moment. The great thing about running, regardless of your time is the camaraderie and people cheering you on. I wanted to do my best because of my father's unintended motivation.

When you work so hard for something, when you achieve that goal, it's pretty powerful stuff.

And to do that with all of my friends around was pretty special.

Boston Marathon bombing 2013

I had decided that 2013 was going to be my last year running marathons. I'd had enough. My knees were crap from torn cartilage. I tore my Achilles tendon from training so hard. My ankle had to be reconstructed from the wear and tear. I'd had four surgeries. I didn't work as hard after that. I was mentally and physically ready to be done running marathons. It hurt too much to keep training. I told my daughter that this Boston Marathon was going to be my last one.

"It has been a great run, but this is going to be it," I told her.

My daughter was studying at Roger Williams University, which was basically right around the corner from Boston College. In talking to Melissa, I suggested that she run the last five miles with me. I thought it would be a great time finishing together.

Around mile 20, Melissa met me near Boston College. Though she wasn't really supposed to do this by BAA rules, she entered the course and began running with me as we planned.

But as we all know that day in 2013 didn't go as any of us planned.

Around mile 22, Melissa began receiving text messages asking if we were okay. Neither of us really new why anyone would be asking such a random question. Of course we were okay. We're Pennington's.

Moments later we saw people running towards us, away from the direction of the finish line.

We continued temporarily and made it to mile 25 when we were told of the bombing and ordered to stop running. To say I was upset was quite the understatement. Being raised by a Marine, I don't take "no" very well.

Melissa took charge of Dad at that point. We ended up walking back and sitting on a front lawn in a small neighborhood trying to make sense of it all. After a few hours together, someone came by to pick us up. Safe, battle scarred but none the worse for it. I was pretty upset about it. It was my dream to finish with my daughter and that didn't happen.

Unbeknownst to me, Melissa put it on Facebook that she didn't get to finish with me and decided that in 2014 we would both be returning to finish the marathon. We trained together and would be running not just the finish, but the entire race as father and daughter.

She was now a senior at Roger Williams and she was nervous. It was to be her first marathon.

Training and being part of a team was healing for her. She'd had a series of concussions previously and she doesn't do well in crowds.

Even though I'd run the marathon 22 times, 2014 was a chance to do the Boston Marathon with my daughter. I'd never have an opportunity to do this again.

We started in the last wave. Melissa was extremely nervous of the crowds, but we befriended some big fellas. Scott and J.C. Marsh formed a "V" and protected little Melissa, who was 5 foot, 5 inches and 110 pounds, for the first five miles.

Channel 5 even put together a documentary on us with a collage of pictures of all the things we've done together since she was a baby.

Finishing that marathon together was filled with mixed emotions. I was scared to cross the finish line because I didn't want it to be over.

It was so fulfilling to come down Boylston Street. That's the last marathon I've ever done but it was among my most special, running it with my daughter.

John Dehart

I was living in New Jersey at the time and training with John Dehart when we decided to run in the New York City Marathon in 1984. He was slower than I was at the time. I was wearing a "Go John Go" T-shirt and wanted to cheer John on. It was 85 degrees on the streets of New York City and I decided to cut holes in my T-shirt.

John ended up dropping out at mile 4. I was determined to finish though. Along the way, I met this young African-American man named Howard around mile 15 near the Queensboro Bridge. It was so hot, we decided to take our time as we ran along 1st Avenue. A couple miles later, we entered Harlem.

Bill, Greg and Melissa on the Boston Marathon course

"I got you through 1st Avenue, Howard. You get me through Harlem," I said to him.

"You stay behind me then," he said.

That's the funny thing about marathons. You become friends with strangers so quickly. I felt bad for John for dropping out, but it was a great opportunity to get to know Howard. I never saw him again after that, but I still have my "Go John Go" T-shirt.

A Devil with so Much Heart
Susan Hurley

If you are lucky enough to train for and run the Boston Marathon, you will be greeted at mile 16 by the Devil. Not the typical demon you might face when beginning your trek through the toughest part of the Boston Marathon, the hills of Newton. I'm talking about a real person. In fact, not a devil at all,

although that is what he has been nicknamed. Bill Pennington is the DEVIL.

Bill has been working as a committed coach to Charity Teams runners of the Boston Marathon for about thirteen years. His nickname was given to him by a group of runners who felt that their hill workouts on the Boston Marathon course were like going to "hell and back". Bill has been instrumental in preparing runners to face their fears and to be confident in running this 5-mile stretch of road. Bill has tried to "break' each runner but, through his challenges, these runners grow strong and gain the confidence they need to make the turn at the fire house in Newton and confidently push up the hills.

Bill has a variety of ways he likes to champion a runner's confidence. He often gives out popsicle sticks that say "no breaking "and red rocks which remind runners that the "rocks and roots" will get you there. He's also been known to blind fold runners or have them carry large sticks up a very steep incline he deemed "The Devil's Den". Every unconventional running challenge he creates has a distinct purpose in the preparation to run the Boston Marathon.

Ten weeks of hill training culminates with a graduation ceremony with the Devil. He is notorious for his stories but on this night, he expressively reads his own version of the Herb Brooks pregame speech for the USA Olympic Hockey team. He presents runners with handmade certificates to commemorate their efforts and acknowledge "the will to prepare."

Bill is someone we love to hate. But when he suffered a severe heart attack a few years ago, his Charity Teams disciples showed up in droves to offer their support and push him through his own challenges. We owed it to Bill to do just that. We would not be who we are without

Bill. He is a fixture in our running community and his inspirational stories of how others overcome their demons motivates us all to be our very best not just on race day, but in life. There been a "Devil" with so much heart.

Susan Hurley – Founder of Charity Teams

That Voice in Your Head
John Young

I first met Bill Pennington way back in the mid 2000's. I am a teacher at a small prep school on the north shore near Boston and Bill's son was in my math class. We got to know each other through that relationship and then years passed until we connected again around 2013, when I was about four years into my journey as a triathlete and marathoner preparing to run my first Boston marathon.

A little history about what led me to be an endurance junkie. I grew up with achondroplasia, the most common form of dwarfism. I had always been told as a young kid not to run because doctors thought it would be bad for my back. Fast forward to 2007 or so and there I was a 40 year old out of shape dad, struggling to get healthy.

After being encouraged by my wife to get to the doctor, I weighed in at 195 lbs. and was diagnosed with severe sleep apnea. After being prescribed a CPAP machine, I started to get some proper sleep and got back into swimming. I then took up cycling to work (ten miles each way) a couple of times a month. Then one day a good friend sent me a video of Dick and Rick Hoyt doing an Ironman triathlon and I got an idea. Maybe I could complete a sprint triathlon. So in 2009, I signed up for and completed my first triathlon, the Mill City triathlon in Andover, MA. I was HOOKED!! That summer I completed three more sprint races.

I never had the dream of moving to longer distance races, but that's what happened. In 2010, I did a half-marathon and Olympic distance triathlon. All along the way, I met some amazing people and that's when I was reconnected with Bill. At the time, I was preparing to run in my first Boston marathon in 2013. I was training with Achilles International and managed to run on Saturday mornings in Boston with many of the Boston Marathon Charity Runners. Bill works as a coach with them on Tuesday nights and is out on the course during the peak training times leading up to the big day in April.

On Marathon Monday, Bill positions himself and his support crew just after the Newton Firehall on Comm Ave. His placement is not random as it is a crucial part of the course where many runners need some love and encouragement. Each year that I run, the thought of meeting up with Bill and the others enters my mind just after I leave Wellesley (the 13.1 mile point!). He is a source of support and love but more importantly he also will give you the kick in the pants you need to keep going. There is a reason one of his nicknames is "The Devil". He's that voice in your head, that makes sure you don't relax and stop! Some years it's just a high five, or a cold towel, or maybe a fresh set of gloves and of course snacks as well. But this one year, I wasn't having the race I had hoped for and was content to just walk the course. Bill gave me the biggest hug and I knew all was good. Bill helped me realize that I still had some running left in me and I was able to keep going, with a lot

more effort than I thought I had left. Bill reminds all of us that there is
#NoBreaking

John Young

Glenn Sauder and Bill
Feet Didn't Touch the Ground for 26.2 miles

Chapter 3
Never Missed a Day of School and Then This Happened

Growing up, I never missed a day of school. I had perfect attendance from kindergarten through my senior year of high school. I was never sick. It wasn't until 2014 that a series of health issues started to arise.

Twisted ankle

Throughout my athletic career, I have sprained my ankle about 30 times. Working on a golf course, the possibility of spraining an ankle on a rock or a hole is very high. Once you start to sprain your ankle, the ligaments aren't as tight as they used to be. I went to see orthopedic surgeon Dr. John Boyle prior to running a marathon in 1992 and he bandaged it up to provide support so that I could run.

Afterward, I had stretched out the ligaments so severely I needed surgery. I thought we'd be able to do the operation with local anesthesia because I wanted to watch it. Dr. Boyle agreed, initially at least. But I guess I was an out-of-control patient as I was talking too much. Eventually, Dr. Boyle put me under and cut me off from being a spectator.

He ended up putting several screws in and everything has been fine ever since. He has performed four surgeries on me in all. After each, I was still able to run marathons again.

Torn Achilles

In January 1993, I was playing a basketball game and felt like someone stabbed me in the back of my calf. Despite the pain, I just went to bed that night and thought nothing of it.

The next day, I hopped on the exercise bike and it still felt weird and made me a little unsure if I should see someone. I ended up calling my physical therapist Andy Cannon at Cedardale Health & Fitness.

"Bill, just squeeze your calf. It will cause your Achilles tendon to move your foot," said Cannon.

I did and it didn't hurt but also didn't contract.

Charlie Blatchford member of charity team

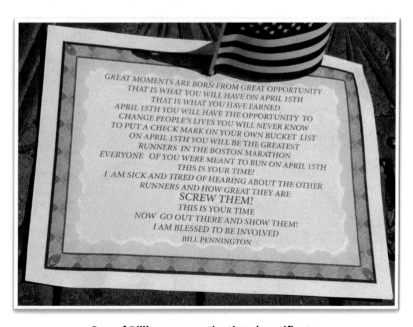

GREAT MOMENTS ARE BORN FROM GREAT OPPORTUNITY
THAT IS WHAT YOU WILL HAVE ON APRIL 15TH
THAT IS WHAT YOU HAVE EARNED
APRIL 15TH YOU WILL HAVE THE OPPORTUNITY TO
CHANGE PEOPLE'S LIVES YOU WILL NEVER KNOW
TO PUT A CHECK MARK ON YOUR OWN BUCKET LIST
ON APRIL 15TH YOU WILL BE THE GREATEST
RUNNERS IN THE BOSTON MARATHON
EVERYONE OF YOU WERE MEANT TO RUN ON APRIL 15TH
THIS IS YOUR TIME!
I AM SICK AND TIRED OF HEARING ABOUT THE OTHER
RUNNERS AND HOW GREAT THEY ARE
SCREW THEM!
THIS IS YOUR TIME
NOW GO OUT THERE AND SHOW THEM!
I AM BLESSED TO BE INVOLVED
BILL PENNINGTON

One of Bill's many motivational certificates

"Bill, don't bother, it's completely torn," he told me. "It's completely ripped and you're going to have to have surgery."

So, I called Dr. Boyle, who was in Texas at the time. He told me I ought to come see him, so he could take a look at it. My biggest concern though, to his surprise, was whether or not I could do RAGBRAI in July.

Dr. Boyle said that I could probably ride if I made sure not to stand on my bike. He did stress that he preferred that I have time to fully recover but told me that as long as my foot never touched the ground while it was in the cast, I should be alright.

Again, I was interested in being awake for the surgery. When you're an athlete, you're interested in understanding how everything works. Dr. Boyle came in on his Harley, all dressed in black. Everyone thought we were nuts. And maybe we were.

I was doing the stay-at-home dad thing at the time. Both of my kids were phenomenal and so understanding about the whole thing. For eight straight weeks, my cast never touched the ground.

By April, I started to put weight on it and gradually took steps here and there, and then on the bike. In July, I rode across the state of Iowa. Dr. Boyle said he's never seen something heal like that. I've never had a problem since.

Skin cancer

In 1995, I went to see dermatologist Dr. Jeremy Finkle two weeks before RAGBRAI. I was extremely lucky. Dr. Finkle discovered that I had skin cancer that was ready to set down its roots, but he managed to dig it out from the top of my head.

Naturally, the first thing I was worried about was making sure I could go to RAGBRAI. Dr. Finkle wasn't too keen on my going to Iowa.

He noted that the area might actually get pretty wet because of sweat. With stitches there, he said that wouldn't be ideal for the area to properly heal.

"It's at the top of my head, Doc," I said to Dr. Finkle. "Doesn't water flow downhill? … I have to do this race."

Dr. Finkle knew I was pretty determined and made me sign a release. I managed to pull it off, but the argument still makes perfect sense to me.

Bladder cancer and a dozen yellow roses

In the fall of 2014, a series of much-more serious issues began. I had been seeing my primary care physician, Dr. Sayeeda Rahman. She knew that I ran all the time and when she noticed that there was blood in my urine, she didn't take it lightly. Dr. Rahman decided to have it checked. I was referred to a urology specialist in North Andover. The experience with the specialist, Dr. Liam Hurley, was not a very pleasant one. In fact, it was very painful. Dr. Hurley ended up finding a tumor. It was small enough though that he was able to remove it.

"Someone is watching out for you," Dr. Hurley said.

This kind of tumor, he explained, isn't usually detectable until it's too late. Had this tumor not been detected, it had the potential to become life-threatening.

I ended up sending a dozen of yellow roses to Dr. Rahman. I'm very grateful for her. A lot of people never find out they have a tumor like this until it becomes very serious. In my opinion, she saved my life.

Mohs surgery

I've spent a lot of time in the sun on golf courses. After seeing dermatologist Dr. Christine Anderson in Andover, she noticed a black spot on my forehead. She referred me to dermatologist Dr. Christine Hayes. While sitting in the waiting room, I noticed via her diploma hanging on the wall that she had earned her doctorate from the University of Iowa. Based on my experience with people from Iowa, I knew from that point on, I would be okay. And I told her that.

The cancer was roughly an inch-and-a-half long by an inch-and-a-half wide.

The specialist performed a surgical technique known as Mohs micrographic surgery or "Mohs surgery" in February of 2015. In the surgery, thin layers of the cancer-containing skin are removed. She ended up having to go in twice to make sure it was all removed. I was lucky as the cancer was benign. I still have an indentation in my skull from this one.

Heart attack

I was running a lot and in really good shape in 2015. On May 7, I ran ten miles in the afternoon. Later, I attended a sold-out Tom Brady engagement at Salem State University with Kerry and Alison Phelan, my girlfriend and her daughter, respectively. There were between 3,000 and 4,000 people in attendance at the event and it was fairly warm. I noticed people started to fan themselves and I started to sweat a little, but not much. Then my hands felt numb, like they fell asleep, and I started not to feel well. I was convinced it might be the heat but was curious why no one was reacting the way I was. I was in better shape than they were.

When Tom Brady finished speaking, I got up and managed to get outside. I thought I might be dehydrated. When I went back to Alison's house, my hands were still numb even as I started rotating my arms around. Kerry, who has knowledge of health and anatomy, looked at me and told me that she thought something was wrong. She suggested I go to the walk-in clinic to figure out what was going on with my hand.

I was a little nervous because I lost a couple friends to heart attacks and sudden-death situations. My blood pressure is usually 160 over 110 and my pulse is usually in the low 50s. But when it was tested, while I was just sitting there, my pulse was 90 and my blood pressure was 170 over 120. Shortly after, they hooked me up to perform a stress test and performed an ultrasound and they told me I was having a heart attack. From there, I was sent to the emergency room at Lahey Hospital & Medical Center in Burlington where they prepared me for surgery.

When I spoke to a nurse, I learned that one of my arteries was more than 90 percent clogged. They wheeled me back and they said my numbers still weren't looking good.

When I woke up, I was greeted by an old-fashioned doctor from New England, who was checking on how I was doing. I asked if I was going to need another stent put in and he said yes.

"Let me understand this," I said to him. "I have two arteries clogged up … I still ran with not one, but two clogged arteries. So if we unclog them, I should be able to run faster than I ran before, right?"

The doctor shook his head in the negative.

"What did we even do this for if I can't run faster?" I asked.

He said that in his entire 50 years of practicing medicine, he'd never heard a response like this.

I ended up having two stents put in. My ability to run faster though is still up for discussion.

The whole experience proved to truly be a blessing. I can't tell you how many people came to visit me. Two of the runners I coached, Kevin Koncilja and Julie Cashman, came up on a Sunday around noontime. They had four kids at home, but still didn't leave until 9 p.m.

The experience made me value every single day more than I ever did before. I think the experience made me understand and really appreciate my friends. I'll always be grateful for that.

Pacemaker

In 2015, I learned that my heart beats irregularly and had atrial fibrillation or AFib. The condition has the ability to lead to blood clots, stroke, heart failure or other complications. At least 2.7 million Americans are living with AFib, according to the American Heart Association. For two weeks, I had my heart monitored to see what's going on.

Two weeks passed and I sent my monitor in. The doctor that read my report asked if I was okay. He mentioned that for some reason, my heart was stopping at night for a few seconds at a time.

Dr. Gautam Gady indicated that I would be alright, but I would need a pacemaker. In that discussion, he started laying out a timeline for when the procedure to install a pacemaker might be taking place. It didn't make sense to me because I had a lot of desirable bike rides that I wanted to participate in over the summer.

I decided to talk to my friends that were nurses at Lahey Hospital. They encouraged me to call straight away if I had symptoms.

I really wanted to go to Iowa but knew that the installation of the pacemaker wouldn't take place unless I had symptoms. So, I called and two days later, I had my pacemaker installed.

My cardiologist was worried about my falling especially because I was on blood thinners, including Warfarin, aspirin and Plavix. They were worried that if I crashed, I would bleed to death. But eight weeks after the installation, I went to RAGBRAI and I was fine.

Staph infections

Alison and I were training to do a half marathon in September. I had pain in my lower leg that felt like sciatic nerve pain. Around Labor Day in 2015, it felt really bad and I ended up at Lahey Hospital again. They checked everything. Being raised by a Marine, I thought I'd be fine if I just took a shower. I figured it was just a pinched nerve.

But I didn't feel better. It felt worse and I started to really shake. Brooke ended up taking me to the hospital.

I had a temperature of 104 degrees. I was prescribed antibiotics. I had some severe lower back pain and I was told I had a staph infection. Honestly, I didn't know the difference between a staph infection and a toenail infection at the time.

Doctors told me that my body was not handling the infection very well. They scheduled me for an MRI. I was worried about laying on my back since I was in so much pain. Doctors indicated that the scan could take up to two hours.

You have to understand I was in big time pain. They were giving me high levels of painkillers. I ended up requesting that they just give me Tylenol because I don't like being on painkillers. I think they ended up giving me about 2,000 milligrams of Tylenol.

In the end, to get through the MRI, I pretended I was running a marathon. Every half hour I equated to running five miles. I talked it out while I was being scanned. Doctors had no idea what I was talking about. An hour went by and I said I was on mile ten.

An hour and a half went by and enduring it became more difficult. It got hilly.

By the time I had fifteen minutes left to go, I said something one of my biggest fans used to say. It was something that was said in during the fight that occurred as passengers attempted to overtake the hijackers on Flight 93.

"Let's roll," I said, while lying there in severe pain.

Afterward, the doctor said, "I don't know how you did that."

The medical assistant asked what I needed once I was through and I requested massive amounts of ice. He took off and left me in the hallway.

He returned a short time later with four bags of ice and tossed them on my back.

I had that staph infection for the entire month of September. I shot myself up with antibiotics and had to give myself drugs three times a day. It was a tough year, but I fully recovered from it.

Bladder problems

I continue to have my bladder checked. In 2018, I had my bladder inspected and the results showed that it was normal. Dr. Hurley examined it again in December 2018.

I'm not sure what happened, but something is going on," he said. "It's rather inflamed."

He instructed me to drink cranberry juice and see how it goes. He said by January I'd have to have a biopsy scheduled. He examined everything and I was fine.

The problem was the fact that I was on blood thinners. I was watching a pro golf tournament played at Pebble Beach with my son Greg and there was blood in my urine. It scared the livin' daylights out of me. I wasn't sure if I would have to fly home. I called Dr. Gady and he calmed me down by sharing the flashlight story with me. He compared the effects of a little blood turning my urine red to a small flashlight in a dark room lighting up the entire room. The appearance was far more than the actual issue.

I used to get nosebleeds that lasted eight to ten hours. I never had them until I started taking all of those blood thinners. With an irregular heartbeat, if my heart paused, clots would form in the heart.

My cardiologist stressed the importance of living every day and got me motivated to start thinking like that. I managed to lose 20 pounds and get even healthier in the following year. The whole thing might have been scary at first, but it motivated me to be better than I had been.

Chapter 4
Life on the Green

Ever since the eighth-grade, I had a love and fascination with greenhouses. My first love was with plants growing in the greenhouses. My father built one in our backyard. In 1969, I was making $1.10 an hour working in a greenhouse.

Then I started caddying at golf courses making a whopping $10 for only four hours which marked a huge pay increase. I had to sign in around 6 o'clock in the morning. I didn't like waiting around, so I volunteered and would also set up the course. The golfers didn't start playing until 10 a.m. It was quite an enjoyable experience.

My friend Dan Shannon and I would caddy together. I knew the balls that my two golfers, Dr. William Kelly and Dr. Thomas Nally, used to play with. Dan and I would compete to see which of the golfers we'd caddy for would have a better round. It was a friendly bet of $1 or $2. I continued caddying through college.

Both Dr. Kelly and Dr. Nally were professors at the University of Rhode Island. In 1973, they had a program in golf course management and I thought I would apply there. It wasn't as difficult to get into the university back then. I asked Dr. Kelly and Dr. Nally how I should apply to get into the school in April of 1973. They told me they'd bring me an application the next weekend.

After I filled it out, I handed the application back to them and they told me that I would hear back from the university soon. At the time, I was more interested in sports and caddying than I was in attending college. My high school GPA and SAT scores weren't very high, but their recommendation helped out a lot.

I ended up getting my acceptance letter a week later. The program I was signing up for didn't have a lot of applicants. I ended up achieving the Turf Grass Student of the Year honor as the top student from around the country. I was gifted an all-expense paid trip to Racine, Wisconsin, home of Jacobson Turf Equipment. Most of us went on to work at some high-end courses following graduation.

College days at Quidnessett Country Club

I was acting like a college student, setting up beer wagons and stations to sell things.

When it got dark, we employees knew that no one watched the pool, so we'd go swimming under the stars. One night, we were out fooling around, probably some alcohol was involved, and a friend, Tracy Sullivan, got into the golf carts that weren't locked up properly. While driving a cart, Tracy went over a bunker, which caused him to go airborne. He broke several ribs as a result. His parents sued the golf course for damages and they actually won.

Tim Straight, the best man at my wedding, was watering the golf course one night. What we'd do is jump off of the tractor, while it was running, and run ahead to put the sprinkler on. Typically, you'd leave it in neutral running and then hop back on after.

Tim, however, was deaf in one ear. His bad ear was facing the tractor and he didn't hear that it began rolling down the hill. The tractor tire hit him and it was so heavy that it actually pinned Tim down. He was okay, but it made for a funny story.

Montclair Country Club 1984

After several years of experience working on golf courses, I met this woman, Brooke Mueller, who later became my wife. Brooke worked in New Jersey as the store manager at Macy's department store and suggested I get a job down there as well. I started looking up some courses down there and found one only four miles from where she lived.

I got to know the mechanic, Ryan, at that course and he said he'd tell his boss about me the following Friday after work. He told me to meet him at The Bottom of the Hill Bar, and I brought my resume to his boss, Ed Nicholson.

While there, I drank and ate for free, but still never got any face time with the boss. It was rather comfortable, but I couldn't be sure if I had the job or not.

"When am I going to talk to the boss?" I asked Ryan.

"Bill, you aren't that dumb," Ryan said to me. "Have you paid for anything since you've been here?"

"A formal statement would be helpful, ya know," I said.

Ryan dragged his boss over to formalize the arrangement and he told me I was all set.

My time at Montclair Country Club was such a great experience. We hosted the U.S. Amateur with 36 holes and famous architect Reese Jones was there. There were 30 employees at the time and 24 of them came from Puerto Rico. They would come up in March and work through Thanksgiving. They knew enough English for me to be able to get the basics across to them.

My buddy, Juan, was on the 7th hole cutting around a golf tee when I learned of a storm approaching. Most of the workers liked to finish their work once they started. Believe it or not, the course had no sirens that warned of upcoming thunderstorms. I decided to make hand signals, to advise them of the approaching inclement weather. I motioned to Juan to come in from the storm. And I'm glad I did.

The next day, I showed Juan a big oak tree that was split in half by a lightning bolt. He got on his hands and knees and prayed, "Gracias, Señor," he said.

While at Montclair Country Club, I put down an enormous amount of grass seed in April. From the day I put it down until the meeting I had with my boss, the average temperature actually decreased as we had an extremely cold spring. In order for the seed to germinate, the temperature should be above 60 degrees. Because the temperature was so chilly, none of the grass seed was germinating.

One day, I had a meeting with my boss and Reese Jones, probably one of the best-known course architects in the world.

"Ed, I can't understand why you can't grow grass here," Reese said.

I stood up and said, "The soil temperature needs to be 60 degrees to germinate. When we started it was 62 degrees and the soil temperature has since gone down. When it starts to warm up, it will be in good shape but not much we can do about it until then."

Reese was speechless upon hearing the explanation of a young groundskeeper like me. He just turned and walked away.

My boss took me out that night to The Bottom of the Hill bar. He told me he would never forget what I had done that day. We had quite a night at that bar.

Blue Hills Country Club Interview 1984

My wife had been named the director of the Midwest division and was transferred to Kansas City. I, of course, moved once again with her.

I met golf pro Tom Watson, who became a really good friend of mine. The Kansas City Country Club was a very nice place. I filled out a resume and went undercover. I went as a member and walked around the course taking notes. I dropped off my resume soon thereafter and later knew they had contacted all my references.

I thought I was all set but hadn't heard back. But I kept coming back hoping for a positive update.

At the end of my undercover experience, I told the club, "Ya know guys, I know you've checked out all my references and I've been here several times."

Obviously, I had spent a lot of time there. I knew them and they knew about me. So I said, "You don't make excuses, and I don't accept excuses, so why don't we sign right now and enjoy a beer together?" I was officially hired on the spot following my aggressive close of the sale.

From Kansas City, I went to Bill Spence to ask about job openings and he told me to go to Blue Hills Country Club. It was probably the best job I ever had.

The general manager, Mike, was playing golf and I was working on the 18th green. That guy never got upset. We worked really well together for the most part. One time however, he comes off the 18th green and calls me over with a raised voice.

"Bill, there's too many broken tees out there. We can't have that here," he says.

I responded in a way that I don't think he expected.

"Wow, Michael. Thank you so much," I said. "I really appreciate the compliment."

"The compliment?" he said.

"Think about it, Michael," I said. "If your only complaint is a few broken tees on the 18th hole…is that really the worst news ever? Was that really the worst round of golf you've ever had?"

Michael offered up an apology and asked for forgiveness. He even offered to buy me lunch.

We never fought again after that.

Laying sod Blue Hill Country Club 1985

I used to do a lot of work with people who had drug and alcohol problems and many on the prison release program in Kansas City. I was working with one guy, Larry, and was getting along with him rather well. I couldn't imagine what he had done to end up in jail. His work ethic and disposition were great. So I asked him.

"What are you in for?" I asked.

"Attempted murder," Larry said.

I was shocked.

"Back six years ago, Bill, I was selling drugs. This guy was a couple bucks short, wouldn't pay me and he walked away, so I shot him in the back. He owed me money," Larry said rather matter-of-factly.

I asked him if he had any regrets, but again, he surprised me.

"I feel really bad about it," Larry said. "I should have killed him."

I got the warden on the phone after that and asked him to send someone over as soon as possible. Larry talked about the situation like he went to lunch and had a hot dog.

He seemed like the nicest guy in the world, but not the kind of guy I'd want to cross…or turn my back on … We got along so well too.

Summit Chase Golf Course 1986

My wife and I moved to Snellville, Georgia in 1986, as her work at Macy's brought us to the south. This was the middle of redneck heaven. There were beat-up pick-up trucks and good ol' boys and I'm the newcomer with a Yankee accent. I had only been there about one week when I happened upon a sign in Gwinnett County. The sign said, "N****rs Don't Sleep in this Town Tonight." No Black people were allowed to live in this town. It was a shocking sign to see.

Around the same time, there was a Civil Rights march from a local mall to the courthouse and the KKK, sporting their robes and confederate flags, had planned to shut down the march.

The word got out over Dr. Martin Luther King Jr. weekend that there was going to be a big march. I was intrigued by the whole thing. I believed in the issue of Civil Rights. I said, "Guys, I'm going to check this out."

And they asked what side I was going to march on. Again, I was taken a back.

I wasn't interested in going to march, I just wanted to look around. As I got there, I thought to myself: what have I gotten myself into.

I ended up finding this African-American gentleman that was like 6 foot, 6 inches and 280 pounds, and I stuck by him. He told me to stay with him and make sure I watch the Georgia State Patrol. If the state police turn inwards, they will beat the living daylights out of us.

I couldn't believe it. Looking back on that, it's crazy to see that this resembles what's still happening at times these days.

Black widow

A few weeks after the march, I was still not really accepted yet at Summit Chase Golf Course. Bobby, one of the workers, began telling me about valve boxes in the ground. He told me that I ought to bring matches with me when I go and to light up dead grass in the event that I see any black widow spiders. I told him I'd wear gloves and be fine. I ended up finding four black widows in that valve box.

Later that day, I'm out with a weed whacker and grass trimmer. The course was overgrown with weeds and as I whacked the weeds four or five feet away was a brown snake. I got some rocks and started chucking them at it. After quite a few misses, I yelled to Jimmy the mechanic, "What type of snake is this? If it bit me, how long would I have?"

He responded by saying, "It's a copperhead snake, but there's no hospital around for your Yankee ass."

It was quite an introduction to the south.

Kip Tyler

Kip Tyler was a very meticulous individual and never wanted to be embarrassed. He didn't tolerate any human error. Ever.

I would set up the golf course at Salem Country Club in Peabody, Massachusetts, put tee markers in the right place, take notes and report back to him. Tee markers have to be in line when you play the game of golf.

I'd be flying around doing all this extra stuff and taking these notes. If one of the tee markers was moved and had an outbreak of crabgrass, I wrote it down in my book. It was time-sensitive, so I got back in my golf cart and drove to the next hole but forgetting to move the tee marker back in line.

Kip comes flying up and he's screaming at me.

"I just can't have you working here," he shouted at me.

"Kip, what's the issue?" I asked.

"They'll think I'm a fool for hiring people like you," he says. "Bill, you changed the tee markers on the 11th hole and they're way out of alignment."

"Kip, stop for a minute," I said to him. "We're all human. I made a mistake. It's probably one of the few mistakes I've made since I've been here."

I pointed out how many times Kip had run out of gas on the course since I'd been there.

"So one of these times you run out of gas, why don't we make a big deal about it, I'll scream at you and tell you it's not right?" I said to him.

Kip and I became extremely good friends. He was named the Golf Superintendent of the Year by the Golf Superintendents Association of America and gave me the best compliment I've ever received when he called me one the most conscientious people he's ever met. To exceed the expectations of Kip Tyler meant a lot.

Longmeadow Golf Course, Lowell, Massachusetts

Joe Gallagher, came from Todesco Country Club in Marblehead, and took over as the superintendent of Longmeadow Golf Course in Lowell while I took over as assistant superintendent. Dave Flanagan, a member of the board for the country club, hired Joe, and Joe then hired me. The place had fallen into disrepair. It wasn't well organized or professionally maintained.

I remember the first or second day after we took over, the two of us were using very scientific tools to measure surface temperature. The tools I used measured exactly what the surface temperature of the grass was without any guess work involved. The measurements allowed me to see how much moisture was in the ground, so I can report it back to the superintendent and make really good decisions. With a record like that, you can plot and diagram the green better, so you know how much water to use and where.

Dave asked about some of the specifics and I started to respond with, "I think …" and before I could finish my thought, Dave cut me off with: "I don't want you to guess, I want you to know!"

Prior to us coming on board, the course used to have an individual that worked there that would provide guesstimates. Our method was extremely scientific and precise. My father taught me to measure twice, cut once as he was in construction. I felt confident about the work we were doing.

When Dave inquired about our methods, I snapped back.

"Joe and I don't f**king guess," I said. After that, he left us alone.

Within a year, we had made some tremendous improvements to the course. Joe and I flipped that place really good. It's a really nice course now.

Chapter 5
The Feaster Five Road Race Through the Years

The Feaster Five Thanksgiving Day Road Race has been a tradition based in Andover since 1988. In the beginning, it was a very simple event with no real fanfare. The race was five miles from start to finish and included basic registration forms and a fee of $10 to enter. With that admission, patrons received a short-sleeved T-shirt to commemorate their participation in the race. The idea came to fruition after I had run a race in Atlanta in 1987 on Thanksgiving Day. Despite how popular football is in that area, they still got 4,000 people to participate.

After Brooke and I moved up to Andover, I discussed establishing a race on Thanksgiving Day with the local police department, who were not confident that people would come. They told me that they had concerns that the race would ruin Thanksgiving for everyone. I, on the other hand, was confident that we'd have more people come to the race than would show up at Andover's annual football game against Central Catholic. They weren't convinced. They all looked at me like I was crazy. But as it turns out, I wasn't.

My wife's brother had a fond affection for Special Olympics. He, too, said it wasn't worth getting involved at the time because we were too small. I am, however, tremendously motivated by people that say it won't work, or that people won't come. To me, this seemed like a tremendous opportunity.

The first year was just as we had planned: simple. One of the more unique ideas was borrowed from an Atlanta-based half-marathon. The race provided pies to its runners, so we decided to hand out pies to anyone who averaged an eight minute mile or less. We served pies from

Purity Supreme Supermarket, which Sue Cronin, president of the running club Merrimack Valley Striders, helped secure. Both she and her husband, Bob Cronin, were very helpful. The first year's race was led by co-directors John and Debbie Burke. We had about 400 people participate.

The following year, we had a little more time to plan. Word got out and the event seemed to gather momentum. That year, we again planned to give everyone a pie that completed the entire race in under 40 minutes. It was pretty exciting because we had 900 people pre-registered for the event. But that morning, a nor'easter dumped more than six inches of snow throughout the course.

Ken Mahoney, town manager of the Town of Andover at the time, was not a runner. He could not relate to runners whatsoever and didn't think people would come out in the inclement weather, but I told him that people would run anyways.

Around this time, we were one of only two races in the area on Thanksgiving Day; the other being in Boston. Lucky for us, many that had planned on heading out to Boston decided to remain around Andover instead. Despite the weather, we still had 600 people show up for the race, 80 of which registered that day in person. I think the fact that it snowed on Thanksgiving Day really gave us a kick going into the following year.

1990

A good friend of mine from Kansas City, Dave, who happens to be a psychiatrist and runs for overall fitness and satisfaction, mentioned something to me that stuck with me in 1990. He noted that when you limit giving pies to those who run fast, there's not as much incentive for those behind them. The back of the pack gets forgotten. He suggested I give out pies to the last 1,000 people instead. That excited people because even if you go slow, you're still eligible for a pie.

The year 1990 was also the beginning of the cell phone craze where we could set up mobile phones that came in a bag. We decided to partner with Universal Cellular and promoted that you could call home, free of charge, at one of 25 mobile phone stations around the course.

We also got involved with one of the greatest charities at the time - Lazarus House Ministries. The Merrimack Valley-based nonprofit organization was established to aid in breaking the cycle of poverty by providing food, clothing, housing and work to those in need.

And as Dave McGillivray, an athlete and director of the Boston Marathon, likes to say: "We had some hooks. We had many reasons why people would come." McGillivray also got involved this year as a sponsor.

We also received tremendous support from the Andover Townsman, which ran a special section on our event that extended to 15 pages. Two years later, the special section extended to 26 pages. 1990's special section helped build our credibility with future sponsors. This was a tremendous marketing event for Bernardin Insurance, who was very instrumental in putting the special section together.

So that year, people could get a pie, call home and even get a sweatshirt for running our race. John MacArthur of Stickman Sports also donated gloves with Feaster Five Stickman Sports logo on them. Market Basket took over as the sponsor for the pies. They brought a trailer full of pies and sold them to us for 90 cents each.

When the race started on Main Street that year, we had 1,800 participants. My buddy Bob "Bob the Cop" Cronin had told me that there would be no police protection that morning of the race and that many intersections would go unprotected. But ultimately, we ended up having much of the area covered by volunteers. The event went off very well and helped continue to build enthusiasm for the race.

This year certainly had lots of bells and whistles. We also had a blood drive for a boy that had leukemia in Georgetown. While we weren't able to find a donor for him, we were able to help out two other leukemia patients.

As people completed the race, we learned many people didn't want to be identified as slow and ended up turning down the pies, so we decided everyone would get one moving forward. From that point on, everyone that participates gets a pie.

1991

In 1991, the race participation exploded to 4,000 participants. By the fourth year, we were pretty set financially. We had secured a significant sponsorship from Dave McGillivray Sports Enterprises. Our volunteers had worked hard for the last few years and it was clear that the event had gotten too big for our volunteer running club, but we kept our fingers crossed even as we may have been making mistakes along the way. We must have been doing something right because 4,000 people is 4,000 people. We were also able to contribute between $5,000 and $6,000 to Lazarus House Ministries.

By 1991, we were able to hire a race announcer and some people were getting paid. Overall, 90 percent of those connected with the race were still volunteers.

As for prizes, I'm not sure we could pull it off in the same manner these days. Our top male finisher, Guy Stearns, won use of a Porsche for a weekend. Our top female finisher, Nancy Peterson, well, she received a Christmas tree.

"He gets a Porsche and I get … what?"

To this day, she has never let me forget what she won.

1992

In 1992, Johnny Kelley appeared as an honored guest at the start of our race. He was 84 at the time. This was the same year he ran his last full Boston Marathon. In his lifetime, Kelley, a native of Medford and a long-distance runner who represented the U.S. at the Summer Olympics in 1936 and 1948, began 61 Boston Marathons and completed 58 of them.

Kelley was accompanied by 10 nurses from Lawrence General Hospital to protect him from anyone who approached him. He also donated two paintings that we awarded to the top male and top female finishers.

This was also the first year that walkers were allowed in the race. In all, we had a total of 4,500 runners and 500 walkers. As such, we were able to provide a larger donation to Lazarus House Ministries.

We had some quality sweatshirts by then and it was pretty exciting that Dick and Rick Hoyt were going to be able to attend. Jack Fultz, who won the 1976 Boston Marathon under extremely high temperatures, and Andy Cannon, a well-known local physical therapist both appeared at the Expo.

Market Basket was again our source for the pies. At the time, my kids were 4 and 5 years old, and were very good-looking and charming. So I would stroll into Diane Callahan's office at Market Basket with the kids and schmooze. Callahan ran the bakery and she was single and adored my children. Whenever I had to discuss pies, they would go in with me and sit in her lap.

As the event continued to grow, I realized I couldn't keep doing it. I was a stay-at-home dad that wanted to get more involved with the kids' school.

The headquarters for Marshall's, Inc. was located in Andover. Its CEO and president, Jerry Rossi had a number of his staff that would participate and volunteer in our event. Marshall's had also become a big sponsor. Now that they were involved, the start and finish was located in front of the store. When I'd concluded that I couldn't do it anymore, I walked into Jerry Rossi's office and told him. He suggested that I reach out to Dave McGillivray about it. For me, it was important that Lazarus House Ministries continued to be a beneficiary to our annual endeavor. After talking to him, it was a done deal and Dave McGillivray Sports Enterprises took over.

1993

A couple months later, McGillivray took over and I helped out behind the scenes. There was a slight hiccup in that the buyer for the pies, Keith Moore, thought he could obtain the pies for nothing. He thought a lot of himself. When he reached out to me about it, I told him, I said, "Keith, I've done my best. We've been getting a very good price on the pies. I suggest we keep working with Market Basket."

I was still volunteering but had backed off a bit.

About a month before the race, McGillivray calls me up and says that Moore is blowing the whole deal with the pies and asked me to speak to Callahan.

So I bring my kids in to see Callahan and she says, "Hey Bill. What's the story with these pies? That new guy is a real jerk."

I asked if we could just do the same deal, we've been doing all along and she was fine with it.

"We're all set, Bill," she said.

Other than that, it was a pretty easy transition. For the next five years, St. Ann's Home Inc. in Methuen, special education school, and Lazarus House Ministries were the beneficiaries of the money that the race produced.

In the sixth year, I heard a lot of compliments from people about McGillivray. People like Joan Benoit were really impressed with the little details he would add along the way like salting and sanding the water stops.

To this day, it continues to be a very successful race.

Chapter 6
Honoring Our Heroes with Run for the Troops

Run for the Troops MA, D.B.A. Run for the Troops 5K, is a tax-exempt, nonprofit organization, located in Andover. This organization was initially formed to help Homes For Our Troops build and donate specially adapted custom homes for severely injured post-9/11 veterans.

When I decided to run the Boston Marathon, I chose to run in support of a charity, since it was nearly impossible to qualify for the race in my age group. I saw that Homes For Our Troops was one of the charities, so I decided to host a 1-mile loop fun run and pancake breakfast to meet the fundraising requirement. Based on the success and overwhelming community support we received for this event, The Run For the Troops 5K emerged. We raised $8,000 and 200 people ended up attending.

Since many members of my family are veterans, I decided to dedicate the event to them. My mother is a Marine and my father served 30 years in the Navy. Other family members that served are Scott Larson and Glen Pennington, Charles Pennington, Craig Pennington and Hank Jorgensen.

My desire to continue to honor our veterans and to support them is fueled by the knowledge of the sacrifices of my family and all of our veterans.

Each April, we hold a 5K walk/run and a community dinner and silent auction to honor our veterans. In addition to raising funds, these events raise awareness of the needs of our soldiers. The public often forgets the hard human cost for a few to maintain freedom for us all.

To date I estimate that Run for the Troops has raised approximately $150,000 for Home For Our Troops. We could not have done this without the efforts of many, but a tip of the cap needs to go to Peter Clark of Randstad Technologies in Andover, MA, who has spearheaded the efforts and has been a driving force since the beginning.

On top of raising funds to benefit Homes For Our Troops, our mission has expanded to support veteran services provided by Ironstone Farm and Homeland Heroes Foundation. This year, despite the pandemic and the challenges that go along with running the event virtually, we anticipate donations and sponsorships exceeding $30K to go to Homes For Our Troops.

We are helping to build a new house for veterans who come for their retreats at Ironstone Farms. Run to Home Base operation located in Charlestown works with Ironstone farms on weekends. In 2021, the house will be complete providing veterans with a stay at facility while getting therapy to deal with their PTSD.

Run for the Troops will have contributed to the game room along with donations from TD Bank. I estimate we have raised approximately $30K over the years for the veterans' home and veterans' program at Ironstone Farms.

We've also contributed to purchase hand cycles for veterans along with generous gifts from Schneider Electric, Ironstone Farms and Home for Our Troops.

Marine Sgt. Joseph Smith

Marine Sgt. Joey Smith was our target the first year in 2011. He was a phenomenal ambassador and a tremendous guy.

He was a member of the U.S. Biathlon Team, competing in archery, hand cycling, swimming and shooting. He completed his first Marine Corps Marathon on his hand cycle in 2009. Before his injuries, Joey was a boxer for both the Army and the Marines and appeared on HBO in a boxing tournament in 2002.

We held a dinner two days before the run in 2011. More than 200 people attended our event. I was told that the capacity was 200 and we sold out really easily. Texas Roadhouse was supplying the food and the layout of the dining room was based on information we were provided, but we didn't realize that the 200 number included people standing. So what was actually considered sold out was 160 people. Luckily, I had a few friends on the select board that told me they saw nothing and not to worry about a thing.

We served pancakes, sausages and orange juice as part of the event. I was only required to raise $3,000, but I raised more than two and a half times my requirement with $8,000. Through the efforts of Homes For Our Troops volunteers, donors and sponsors, Joey received the keys to his Thomasville, North Carolina home in October 2011. The Homes For Our Troops provides homes for soldiers that make life a lot easier -- from voice-activated equipment to roll-in showers and customized kitchens.

In the years that followed, Joey came up to Massachusetts for the Run for the Troops Dinner and Walk. I looked forward to seeing him and he was trying to regain the ability to walk.

He was paralyzed in Afghanistan. We met in private as he wanted to show me how far he'd come in that quest. He had some movement in his legs and got motivated to try to walk to get Joey a Purple Heart.

He sustained a spinal cord injury and traumatic brain injury in an attack at his Forward Operating Base while serving in Afghanistan in November 2004. Joey never received that purple heart. Somehow the villagers in Afghanistan got on top of the building and put some kind of container on him and paralyzed him.

Seeing the image of the Purple Heart was the most Joey had reacted since his stroke, Debbi said. Unfortunately, ten days later, my dear friend had another stroke and passed away, but I'm glad we could make his day a bit brighter.

Words from an Indebted Military Wife
Debbi Smith

The first time Joe and I met Bill Pennington was at a small Mexican restaurant in Andover, MA. Joe was in disbelief that an organization would build him a home that would allow him to be independent again (Operation Enduring Freedom home!

Before I go further, I must tell you the fact that we were flown to Boston, provided a beautiful hotel room, meals, and entertainment blew Joe away. Why Bill picked Joe to start his foundation, I'll never know but it created a lifelong friendship between the two. You see, when Joe was initially injured in Afghanistan in 2004, he never had one soul visit him (please know we had not met at this time), help him, or care whether he lived or died. Bill changed all of that when he decided to start his fundraiser and picked Joe as a recipient. Someone cared enough to make a difference and say, "thank you for your service to our country. Your sacrifice means something to me." Joe cried tears of joy about that.

Bill instantly made an impact on Joe. He was quiet, kind, and one hell of a patriot. His patriotism made a big impact on Joe. Knowing Bill's mother was a Marine didn't hurt either. During our meal, Bill and Joe made plans to "tour" Andover the next day. They went to several businesses and spoke about what this meant to Joe. Well, Joe spoke, because once he started, he was hard to get quiet! I'm sure Bill didn't get many opportunities to talk.

Our home was completed in late 2010. Joe was shocked at the number of volunteers who helped us through the whole process, but the one that made the biggest impact was Bill Pennington.

They remained friends and stayed in contact up until Joe's death in August 2017. Bill provided Joe a much needed friendship and brotherhood that he missed after retirement from the military.

I'll never forget the day they buried Joe in Arlington National Cemetery, Bill flew down from Andover to be there and say goodbye to his friend. I was not at all surprised he would make a trip like that for one day, because that is who Bill is.

I know Bill wanted a funny story, but I wanted to share what Bill's selflessness and love meant to Joe. It's a friendship and a bond that made a lifetime impact on Joe. He no longer felt alone.

Debbi Smith
Former wife, always a friend to Sgt. Joseph C. Smith
USMC, US Army Retired

Marine Sgt. Joshua Bouchard

On July 8, 2009, Marine Sgt. Joshua Bouchard was on his second deployment when he lost his left leg and broke his back after his vehicle drove over a pressure plated improvised explosive device in Helmand Province, Afghanistan.

While out on a night mission, Joshua and four other Marines were injured in the blast. Two of his team did not survive their injuries.

Ejected from the vehicle, Joshua's left leg was severed by the gun turret, causing a traumatic amputation. When he hit the ground, his back was broken by the impact and he sustained a traumatic brain injury. Lifesaving measures were performed and a tourniquet applied by one of his injured comrades helped stop his loss of blood.

A British Royal Marine performed a direct person transfusion onsite to keep Joshua from dying on the battlefield. Unconscious, Joshua was treated at a local hospital before being airlifted to Landstuhl, Germany, where he spent two weeks being stabilized for transport to Bethesda Medical Center.

Two weeks later, he arrived at McGuire VA Medical Center in Richmond, Virginia, and began his intensive rehabilitation, spending 11 months in therapies before being transferred to Walter Reed Army Medical Center.

Joshua, who is from Granby, MA was our 2012 target. I talked to the fire department and Joshua's parents, Jim and Sue Bouchard, helped organize the event. The event was two hours from Granby and we made sure to provide transportation for the family.

What we tried to do in Homes for Our Troops was find a vet locally, but unfortunately, Josh wasn't mentally ready to come. A lot of these veterans do not like to get thanked or be on display. The day of the event, we went to Granby to meet with the fire department, and 60 residents, including 35 firefighters came out in various degrees of fire gear. We had a huge flatbed truck with banners of Josh to let it be known that the proceeds from this event would be going to Josh's house in Granby.

Sue Bouchard, Josh's mother, was in shock that so many people would be in support of her son. We all embraced.

"If you don't stop crying, I won't be able to pull this event off," I told Sue.

Sue and Jim and I have remained good friends.

U.S. Sen. Scott Brown also attended the event. During his speech, he never mentioned anything about being a senator. He was tremendous and it really helped with the publicity as well. The run had 1600 registered runners.

Marine Cpl. Kevin Dubois

Marine Cpl. Kevin Dubois was on his second deployment when he lost both of his legs at the hip after stepping on an improvised explosive device (IED) in Helmand Province, Afghanistan on July 31, 2011.

While in the role of scout sniper, Kevin was clearing a helicopter landing zone for the medical evacuation of an injured teammate. Upon going into a prone position, his left foot hit the pressure plate of an IED, triggering the bomb. Knocked unconscious by the blast, the helicopter that was previously dispatched arrived soon after the event, airlifting both Kevin and his injured teammate to Camp Bastion.

Next airlifted to Bagram Air Force Base, Kevin required 14 units of blood in order to be stabilized for transport to Landstuhl, Germany. He was airlifted stateside to Walter Reed National Military Medical Center in Bethesda, Maryland before being transferred to Balboa Hospital in San Diego.

Kevin's year was special in many ways. Both Joshua Bouchard and Joey Smith attended Kevin's dinner. It's one of the greatest feats that I've ever pulled off. Kevin was moving from Coventry to Burrillville, Rhode Island. We had 30 people from Burrillville attend that were set up at three tables up front. Kevin was also up front and seated with members of the committee. When we introduced Kevin, we asked that all his new friends and neighbors stand up. At those three tables were all his new neighbors with baskets filled with restaurant and car wash gift cards and other luxury items.

Whenever Kayla, Kevin's wife, and Kevin would talk about anything, they'd say "we." They were quite a couple. It was never one or the other. They gave each other so much credit for everything.

By the 2013 Run for the Troops event, the dinner had gotten bigger too. In 2013, we held it at the Wyndham Hotel. The dinner had become an opportunity to say thanks and support other veterans.

U.S. Army Sgt. Chris Gomes

On Oct. 29, 2008, U.S. Army Sgt. Chris Gomes, a heavy equipment operator with the 54th Engineer Battalion, was convoying back to his base in southern Baghdad, Iraq, when his vehicle was struck with four explosively formed projectiles. The blast resulted in the loss of his right leg and severe damage to the left.

Before arriving at Walter Reed Medical Center, Chris was treated in Baghdad Combat Support Hospital and Landstuhl, Germany. He endured ten surgeries as an impatient at Walter Reed. A month after his arrival, he began outpatient therapy until June 2009. Since then, he has undergone several surgeries to repair extra bone growth.

Chris, a resident of Freetown, Massachusetts, was the target for the 2016 run, which was a special year in a way. There was a mini-snowstorm that lasted from 7 to 830 in the morning that couldn't have come at a worse time. It was snowing like crazy with a couple inches piling up on the ground. While only two-thirds of those that were registered showed up, there were still more than 2,000 people in attendance. It was a real testimony to the cause. As a result of that snowstorm, we ended up switching the date moving forward to the last weekend of April.

Marine Cpl. Roger Rua

On March 29, 2012, Marine Cpl. Roger Rua was serving with the security platoon attached to the 9th Engineer Support Battalion when the vehicle he was riding in drove over a command detonated improvised explosive device (IED) in Helmand Province, Afghanistan. Roger, a resident of Middlebury, Connecticut, sustained fractures to his spine, femur and sternum, and a traumatic brain injury (TBI) as a result of the explosion.

Initially, Roger was paralyzed from the chest down. Doctors were uncertain if he would ever walk again. But after four months of physical therapy at the VA in West Roxbury, Massachusetts, he was able to stand and eventually walk small distances with assistance. By the time he was discharged, he managed to walk with only a cane.

Although there were significant strides made in terms of Roger's health, his chronic lower back pain and injuries often impact his mobility.

In 2017, Roger was the target of the run. This year, we tried a lot of new things, including a pancake breakfast and The Houston Bernard Band.

We also wanted to land a Blackhawk helicopter at the event. After meeting with town counsel, they indicated that there was no way in the world that the Town of Andover would allow that to take place based on the liability.

As the son of a Marine, I'm not used to accepting the word "no." I knew U.S. Army Col. Kathy Romo from town and spoke with her. She got the military to take full responsibility for the landing of the helicopter. Kathy made it so it was okay to land near Central Park and got the police to approve it.

After the race, people got to check out the helicopter. We did really well that year. We raised an enormous amount of money: $40,000. We had roughly 3,300 people participate in the run.

U.S. Army Cpl. Kevin McCloskey & U.S. Marine Lance Cpl. Matias Ferreira

On June 8, 2008, U.S. Army Cpl. Kevin McCloskey was driving in a convoy with the 506th Infantry Regiment (4th Brigade), 101st Airborne Division, in Logar Province, Afghanistan when his vehicle struck an IED. Kevin doesn't remember much of the incident, but he has been told he saw a pressure board and swerved to avoid it, taking the majority of the blast to himself. The explosion resulted in the loss of both his legs, vision loss in his right eye, burns all over his body and a TBI.

Once he returned to the U.S., Kevin underwent 30 surgeries during his stay at Brooke Army Medical Center.

Matias was born in Uruguay and immigrated to the U.S. by way of Atlanta with his family when he was 6 years old. He joined the Marines at 19 and took his oath to become an American citizen days before he deployed to Afghanistan as a machine gunner with the 1st Battalion, 8th Marines.

Just months into his first deployment in January 2011, Matias lost both legs and broke his pelvis after stepping on an IED in Helmand Province, Afghanistan. Treated by Navy Corpsman and medically evacuated to Bagram Hospital, he was flown to Landstuhl, Germany, and then brought to Walter Reed Army Medical Center. There he underwent several surgeries and aggressive therapies. Months later, he eventually learned to walk confidently on prosthetics, advancing to running and other sports a short time later.

Kevin, a resident of Southampton, Pennsylvania, and Matias, a resident of Smithtown, New York, were both named the targets for the 2018 run. This year we also had a hill challenge. We were able to put timing mats at the base of the hill and top of the hill. Those that crossed the finish line, would win a beer glass from a brewery.

Overall, there was a fairly flat course, but between mile 2 and mile 2 ½ there was a really steep hill. Some people were complaining about how we redesigned the course to include going up this hill.

"Why'd you change the course to have us go up the hill?" they'd say.

Well, the reason we did that is because we wanted participants to think of the people who have to go up the hill in Iraq with 40-pounds pack on their back, sometimes getting shot at as they ascend the climb. Sometimes people forget what this race is about and can't identify what war is all about. This part of the race was a good reminder of why we do what we do.

My father passed away in 2012 and it has always been an honor that my dad's flag flies at the finish line. In 2018, my mother passed away two days before the event. She had suffered from Alzheimer's for eight years. This particular year I had a hard time getting the town departments to decide to put up my father's flag and I was getting very frustrated. Around 9:45 the morning of my mom's ultimate passing, I had this tremendous surge of energy. I had just left the house and told myself I should speak to the town one final time to resolve the flag issue.

I was tremendously motivated and wondered why the town couldn't put up a simple flag. I swung by the town offices and went over to Mark Camero, veterans' affairs officer. I got a phone call as soon as I left there that mom passed away. It was really weird.

On very short notice, Tracy Callahan made a special presentation of my mom and raised a lot of money. Mom now has a brick at Quantico. Tracy announced this at the dinner that night. It all came together just 36 hours before the dinner. Anyone who has seen their mother suffer from Alzheimer's, would understand when I say I felt her with me at those moments, inspiring me.

Now the Marine Corps flag and the Navy flag flies at the finish line.

U.S. Army Staff Sgt. Kevin Campbell

In February 2010, U.S. Army Staff Sgt. Kevin Campbell volunteered for a second tour of duty to Southwest Asia as a supply management specialist with the 157th Air Refueling Wing of the 379th Air Expeditionary Wing. Stationed at Al Udeid Air Base in Qatar, he was tasked to tear down and rebuild body armor. Kevin's responsibilities included lifting 40 pounds of body armor for 13 hours a day. On March 2, 2010, three weeks into his deployment, he ruptured two vertebrae while performing his duties. Additionally, the relentless desert sun caused large painful red sores to spread over Kevin's exposed skin. After seeking medical attention, he returned to duty and worked through his back pain and discomfort of his sores for the final month of his deployment.

It was not until he returned to the U.S. in April 2010 that a dermatologist diagnosed Kevin with Systemic Discoid Lupus and informed him that he must avoid all sun exposure. His spinal cord injury has progressed over the past eight years to paralysis in his lower back and left leg, and he now uses a wheelchair most of the time.

For the 2019 event, Kevin was selected as the target. That year, we tried some new things. We raffled off four hand cycles. Snyder Electric wanted something concrete to show for their sponsorship. They wanted to see where their donations were going.

We had a drawing for a two-year lease on a vehicle. Charlie Dare from Commonwealth Motors has been a very involved sponsor. In 2019, I suggested that we hold a raffle, but Charlie said no. I convinced him that we could pull this off. Ultimately, any veteran that registered for the run was immediately placed into the raffle.

The day of the raffle, I got worried. I thought maybe the prize would go to someone that didn't really need it. As it turned out, I happened to be standing across from the winning veteran as they read off the numbers. I could just tell from the look on his face and how he jumped up that he was beyond excited. I couldn't believe we pulled it off.

We also managed to get the singing trooper, Dan Clarke, to perform. He was very good, very powerful, and had an excellent voice. He also knew how to speak to veterans. He's sung at Fenway and all kinds of veterans' events.

Tracy Callahan and Diana Kiesel Yang put on the dinner for the last three years. Tracy is a dear friend of mine that I know from PTO days and Diana owns Yang's Fitness Center.

It was actually Tracy's suggestion to have our veterans lined up to be thanked. One by one, branch by branch, all of our veterans were thanked. It was very powerful. I was so thrilled.

For so many years, we only had 10 to 12 vets and due to tremendous sponsors, I didn't think it was right to charge vets to come to their own party/dinner. By 2018, we had put together a fundraising form for folks to sponsor veterans' tables for $500 apiece.

2019 really was a pinnacle year. That year, we raised $72,000.

Dinners

Dick and Rick Hoyt spoke at the dinner that was held at the Longmeadow Golf Club the second year. We did well and had a good time.

Melissa Flynn organized the dinner for four years. She was very good too. She took over the dinner for me. I needed someone like Melissa and she did a fabulous job. She was the reason that the dinner went to the next level; she made up for my shortcomings. I tended to go by the seat of my pants, while she was a planner.

I'm good at the "big picture," but not the details. The silent auction took shape, for example. She excelled and was very patient with me. Her organization skills allowed us to expand it to averaging from 200 people to 400 to 500 people.

Doing the Right Thing
Diana Kiesel

I knew about his accomplishments and his passion before I ever met the man. With great enthusiasm, one of our employees and dear friend, Cindy Rayner, raved about all of the wonderful things this man, Bill Pennington, had and was continuing to do for veterans in our community.

Cindy wanted to get us and our members here at Yang's Fitness Center involved with a fundraiser called the Run for the Troops 5K (RFTT). As I listened, I knew we had to get involved. That was 2013 when we hosted the first Troop Challenge where fitness enthusiasts in our community banded together to perform military type exercises to help raise money for RFTT. Throughout our planning process, I had met Bill on several occasions but could not say I knew him. My husband, Alex, and I went on blind faith that we were fundraising for a legitimate cause based on Cindy's recommendation. It just felt right and at the conclusion of the evening of the Troop Challenge, we knew we were doing the right thing. The energy and camaraderie of the participants that evening was unbelievable. We had competitive athletes from different fitness arenas all here for the same cause ... to honor those who have served and to make their lives just a little easier for the sacrifices they had made. Bill attended that evening and in his usual fashion, stayed in the background and observed allowing the "chiefs" to run the show.

It was from there that we hosted our second Troop Challenge the following year and then got involved in organizing and hosting the annual pre-race dinner and silent auction held each year on the Friday before race weekend. As I got to know Bill, I would sometimes shake my head and wonder how he was able to accomplish what he has. For those who know Bill, I'm sure you're shaking your head "yes". He is a true leader but not one who gets inundated with the details. He trusts those he empowers authority to and always believes they "will get it done". That's a hard concept for someone like me who is a Type A. Bill has two sayings that always resonate with me ... "find the right people and the job will get done" and "don't let the few influences ruin the outcome". I think of that often when I am struggling with difficult personalities. I can't say I always understand what Bill is saying to me because his brain is always light years ahead of his words but I can say the man always has his heart in the right place. Glad to call this man my friend.

~ Diana Kiesel

The following are several letters that appeared in the Lawrence Eagle Tribune special section created by reporter Bill Burt as a tribute to the Run for the Troops 5K in 2020.

Bill Pennington asked me to write a letter describing why I support the Run for the Troops:

My name is Christine Stark. I'm an Andover native and a recently retired Army Colonel who has run nine of the ten "Run for the Troops" races. I support this event for a number of reasons, not the least of which is to give back to a community that gives us the very freedom to participate in these activities. I cannot begin to express the personal pride I feel each year as I watch the swell of community support grow exponentially giving back to our service members. I have seen firsthand the devastating effects of combat on our troops-some in my own family-and I'm thankful to have this opportunity to give back.

Seven years ago, several of my Andover high school friends came together and formed the Hometown Warriors team. It's a unique combination of Andover High School graduates, former and current Andover Athletic Coaches, families and most of all veterans. We have veterans and active soldiers from the Army, Navy, Marines, and draw runners/walkers from Florida, New York, Pennsylvania, New Hampshire, Maine, and at one time even two runners from Okinawa Japan. We have service animals and therapy horses who inhabit our runner's tent and always proudly display the Andover High banner. Our team has a shared history and enjoys the opportunity each year to come together, recognizing veterans and supporting the many programs that provide valuable assistance to this group.

Lastly, Bill Pennington does a tremendous job organizing the dinner and run and ensuring the maximum return to the charitable foundations. He is devoted to our Veterans and Service members and makes it easy to fall in love with the event. It has been my pleasure to serve this country and my continued pleasure to support the Run for the Troops 5K.

We look forward to getting back out in person next year!!!!!

Respectfully,
Christine Stark

Hi Bill P and Bill Burt,

In 2016 I heard of Run for the Troops 5K for the first time and knew that I wanted to participate. It was also a great way to get my team at TD Bank involved in our community and as a region. At the time I was the Store Manager for the Groveland, MA TD Bank location and my Store Supervisor, Shannon Lynch (of Haverhill, MA) was a veteran. When I mentioned to her that I wanted to get a TD Bank team together she eagerly jumped in to help promote it to the region.

Over the past five years, the relationship between TD Bank and Run for the Troops 5K has grown. I am so proud to say that TD Bank is a key sponsor of the Silent Auction and Dinner over the years. That is on top of our team participation year over year which has also grown. In the years 2018 and 2019, TD Bank had unofficial remote teams that complete 5Ks in Worcester and Cape Cod, in addition to the team participating in Andover.

I personally am involved because I am an outspoken advocate of Veteran's services and issues. I don't think there is ever too much to give or volunteer for our Veterans or for our active men and women in our armed forces. I am not a Veteran myself, but my hero and the coolest guy I know, my Uncle Jim, was a fighter pilot in the Navy and then in the Air National Guard - Lt. Col. James D "Mac" McGeorge.

Although I am not a Veteran, I am an equestrian and know the healing power of horses. My first riding lesson, at nine years old, was at Ironstone Farm. I have followed and supported Ironstone Farm and the Challenge Unlimited program since then. I love that they have added the Veteran's services to their equestrian programs!

Thank you,
Lauren V Dalis— VP Project Delivery Support,
TD Bank, NA | America's Most Convenient Bank

As both an Army daughter and Army wife, you can say patriotism runs deeply in my veins. Running the Run for the Troops 5k each year is just one small way that I can give back to all of the Veterans that do so much selflessly to protect our freedoms. It is much more than just a race, it's a way to give back to the true heroes. Knowing that I can do something so simple to help provide an amazing home for a Veteran is a no brainer. Each year I look forward to running this race to honor those who currently serve, have served, and the ones who are no longer with us. I highly encourage anyone who wants to be a part of something bigger to run this race! It will truly change your life.

Sarah Ivey

Bill,

You never cease to amaze me..not even a pandemic can stop you. The real success of the virtual race is just wonderful for the troops that are helped, the opportunity given to the runners and the spirit of our Town. I know you don't do this alone, and would be the last one to afford credit to yourself, but you have to own that you are catalyst.

Congratulations, my friend!! I look forward to when we can have that chat and catch up!

Sheila M Doherty, LIA, CIC, AAI
President Doherty Insurance Agency, Inc

Chapter 7
A Man on the PTO?

A Sunday introduction

I was a stay-at-home dad and had two kids, Greg and Melissa. They went to South Street Elementary School in Andover and were supported by incredible staff and teachers. South Street Elementary was recognized with a National Blue Ribbon Schools award and I decided to volunteer to be a part of the PTO. I thought it would give me some adult interaction.

It was a Sunday morning when I decided to head over to the school. I was anxious to meet the Principal, Dr. Eileen Woods. When I arrived, there were people moving around bark mulch on the grounds in front of the school. I walked up the walkaway and someone said, "Eileen," and she turned around with a shovel in her hand.

The principal of the school was there on her own time, on a Sunday morning, helping all these people build a playground. That's how I met her. She embraced parent involvement. It sent the stage for the beginning of a phenomenal friendship.

Baseball

Faith Goldstein taught first-grade. She had a phenomenal reputation and was the wife of Rabbi Goldstein. She was a big Red Sox fan.

Part of her morning message was to report on how the Red Sox did the game before. No matter what, she'd tie it in with basic math and writing, like: how many runs did the Red Sox score?

In the spring, they'd play baseball and I'd volunteer. Faith did it right. She had the kids learn the Star Spangled Banner and even served them up some hot dogs.

Fifty percent of those that participated had never swung a baseball bat in their lives, yet everyone ended up being successful.

"Mr. Pennington, how did you do it?" Faith asked.

"You're Jewish, I'm Catholic - we're a guaranteed success if we work together," I told her.

It was the most rewarding thing. Many years down the road, I'd have kids come up to me and say, "Remember the time I hit a homerun?"

We carried on the tradition for the next six years. It was so much fun and rewarding, and Faith was really into it, too.

This began my parent-teacher involvement.

Tulips

The League of Women Voters had a community reading program that I decided to volunteer with. I brought a book to read to the kids called *Tulips* that was written by Jay O'Callahan. The book is set in Paris. Each spring, Pierre visits Grand Ma Mere, who loves her grandson and tulips. Grand Ma Mere has one of the most beautiful gardens in Paris. With each visit, Grand Ma Mere's staff panics as Pierre is known as something of a trickster. In all the times he visited, he never pranked Grand Ma Mere, but this year (in the book) is different.

To coincide with the reading of the book, I'd give each kid one tulip bulb in a brown paper bag. I never told them what color it was so they needed to plant them to learn the surprise behind the tulip. The class would plant them in the fall outside of Faith Goldstein's first-grade classroom. We would explain how the tulip grew and would inform them when they could expect to see them in the spring.

Years later, some of the kids came up to me and told me they remember me.

"You're the 'tulip person'," they'd say.

I am rich in what it did for the kids and what it did for me.

Cultural Enrichment

The school had a program called Cultural Enrichment. With the program, the school was used to people arranging all the programming. The program would host presenters like a "Bill Nye the Science Guy," but I told Dr. Woods I had a problem with that.

"It doesn't follow the curriculum," I told her. "We should change it to curriculum enrichment. We can bring in people that would complement the curriculum."

And that was the first time I started my rabble rousing. But I got a lot of support from the principal. It was something different than the way it was before.

I was probably the only father staying home with his kids and active in the PTO, but they were extremely welcoming.

Book Fair

After switching to Curriculum Enrichment, there was an opening for fundraising; the ways and means chairperson and I was appointed to fill the role.

Cindy Chromer was a member of The South School PTO and worked as a warehouse engineer for Lotus. She was extremely anal and was a huge supporter of me. She was a dreamer and she put all plans down on paper to me enacted while I was admittedly less detail oriented and more of a wing it type guy.

The PTO used to host this annual book fair that I was now in charge of having taken charge of the fundraising division. Each year, they would set it up on the stage at the school behind the curtains, so that it wouldn't be overly distracting. Parents and children would have about a half hour to peruse books during their library time. But I like to do succeed in abundance at whatever I do and having that small window of time with the books being tucked away from everyone didn't make much sense to me. So I said, "Cindy, let's move the event to the kindergarten lobby."

My reasoning was because those parents are the extremely enthusiastic ones since their children are just entering the world of education. The school had this big lobby outside two kindergarten classrooms and I believed we could capitalize on their enthusiasm.

In working with Scholastic Books, I asked the representative what the record was for sales and she stated that it was approximately $21,000. Previous book fairs that our PTO hosted took in between $5,000 and $8,000 and it ran for roughly five days. There would be one night of promotion, but nothing spectacular.

So, I suggested that we create a book fair display in the lobby. We put up balloons and decorations, which included everything from Mrs. Frizzle from the Magic School Bus book series to the Berenstain Bears. I also had coffee on hand to make it an event. One key detail was putting books at eye level of the children. It made a world of difference.

Cindy told me she loved the ideas and thought that everyone would be on board with the event.

I went to Dr. Woods to tell her what I was doing and she told me that it made all the sense in the world. She told me to go for it.

But, despite all of the positive feedback, I was worried about the PTO board meeting. I needed approval from South Street Elementary School PTO and I knew I would be met with opposition.

I made some brief opening comments, but they kept giving me a hard time regarding the plan.

I told them about serving donuts and coffee and all the display cases. I told them that I think that we can do better than what we've been doing.

Still, they kept giving me a hard time.

"How do you know it will all fit?" they'd ask.

Well, Cindy had produced a 37-page manual for the book fair that included a sketch that was drawn to scale. I happened to have the operational manual in my back pocket. When I passed it on to them, they were all in shock at the intricate details. They had never received anything like this before.

"The floor has tiles that were one-foot by one-foot, so I know they'll fit," I said to the board.

Well, turns out I was right. Parents were instantly on board. We missed the state record by just $1,000.

Sock Hop

As chairman of the Ways and Means committee, I took over the outstanding tradition called the South School Sock Hop as a fundraiser. The PTO was concerned that I would not be able to handle this, but I wasn't concerned in the least.

"I've had more volunteers at the Feaster Five than you have had at this event. Just relax," I told the board. "I got this."

I think that calmed them down.

At the time of the Sock Hop, I was putting on the Feaster Five and managed a race with over 4,000 participants and about 300 volunteers. I wasn't concerned about throwing the Sock Hop.

I secured burgers from McDonald's as I had a friend that worked there. My friend Cindy helped out again and got things organized very smoothly with another floor plan laid out.

I used my contacts with the Feaster Five and reached out to three women I knew well that were all dear friends of mine: Lynn Bleech, Amy Cook and Jaime Rockwell. I asked them to dress up as clowns, make colorful sandwich boards, and make yourself visible. I told them to write in big bold letters: "ASK ME WHAT I KNOW."

"But Bill, we don't know anything," they all said.

Exactly, I told them. I had them buy notebooks and write down all that you don't know. That was the beginning of the out-of-the-box thinking that I brought to South Street Elementary School.

Town meeting

When I got selected for the role, I wanted to re-evaluate how we looked at our opportunities and our fund raising.

We recruited businesswomen, women that didn't want to waste time.

I told them, your job is to make me look good.

"Our monthly meetings will last 59 minutes and 59 seconds," I said. "Our goal is to discuss the issues at hand. I don't want to hear about problems with in-laws, diapers or your future ex-husband. You can discuss that after the meeting."

Every year, there's not enough money for the school. I thought that if we can support this budget, we'll do more than the fundraisers. I wanted to put a bug in their ears.

I even brought on Dave MacGillivray for a presentation and talked about how we can put on bake sales and sock hops and raise roughly $25,000 for the school for the year or we can affect the town meeting. (GREATER IMPACT on a town level by supporting the school budget at town meetings)

The Town of Andover had three boards, the Select Board, Finance Committee and School Committee that would get together and try to reach a compromise and present a balanced budget at the annual town meeting.

This year there was a huge gap. This was an excellent way to get behind the School Committee.

I had asked what would happen if we asked for more money than recommended. Well, they will have to make cuts on the town side versus the schools to balance the budget.

So each school raised money and asked for more money than recommended by the Finance Committee for schools.

We were an independent group of people trying to impact town meeting. Historically, that has not happened.

We hired a lawyer for about $500 to write an amendment to increase the budget for the school. We had our plan in place and we asked for just under $1 million.

This was around 2005 when email was just coming out, so we started to form email lists as we got our campaign ready. This allowed us to evaluate how many supporters we had even before the town meeting began.

Jim Doherty, the town moderator at the time was an old-fashioned New England guy, God bless him. He oversaw the whole meeting and would always try to get people to work together.

Instead of burdening 20 or so people on the PTO, why don't we shift more of that responsibility, I suggested at the town meeting. I suggested an amendment to the article related to the school budget that increased the budget on the town meeting floor.

"Historically Bill, that's not what we do here," Jim said.

"Jim, I believe in democracy, and I can't back down," I said. My father has a purple heart fighting for democracy. If I tell him we didn't get this doing it a democratic way he would be very disappointed. We're going to continue to push."

We knew we had the vote, we were counting them. We knew how to calculate before we presented our article and that the budget line item needed to be increased significantly while reducing that elsewhere.

When asked where the town would find the money to make that increase, I told them that it wasn't my job to figure out where the money comes from.

"The priorities of the town are changing and we all go through changes in our lives. We may start by buying diapers, but then we're buying baseball bats for family," I said.

We wanted to let the people of Andover decide where our tax dollars go. Parents felt empowered.

We had 6,000 students in Andover and figured that if we got four parents per classroom, we were good.

But it wasn't close. In fact, the amendment was approved with an overwhelming margin.

Chapter 8
Good Ol' Fraternity Days

In 1973, I was living in a dorm while attending the University of Rhode Island in South Kingston. My older sister was dating someone from Chi Phi Fraternity. Her boyfriend encouraged me to join and I pledged in the fall. It was a great experience. We had 40 members there on Upper College Road. The road was home to five frat houses. Back then, the fraternities and sororities did things together.

During my time there, I was named vice president of the Inter Fraternity Council which represented all 15 of the fraternities on the campus. My best friend Tim Straight was a member of Phi Gamma Delta and the President of the IFC. Tim also became the best man at my wedding. He was a lot more adventurous than I was then. I was primarily involved by overseeing breaking of rules or regulations as they pertained to social events.

Tim used to organize our fraternity scavenger hunts. It was a good way for incoming freshmen pledges to get to know each other. Brothers would make up a list of items and the frosh pledges would have to work together to find them. Being the turf expert I was, I requested a piece of turf from a gravesite. The gravesite I requested it from was from an alleged ghost that haunts the campus, Will Peckham

According to his headstone in the cemetery on campus, Peckham was born on March 3, 1860 and died July 11, 1884. One legend states that William killed his wife, Nancy, because he thought she was being unfaithful. As such, he was found guilty and sentenced to be hung on the date of his death listed on his headstone. Evidence was uncovered later that proved his innocence. Since then, there have been a number of sightings of his "ghost."

To add to the experience of the hunters, the members of the fraternity and I would tie fishing lines to the old iron gates to the cemetery. We'd hide in the bushes and when the pledges went to grab the grass, we'd eerily close the gates behind them.

On one occasion, seeing as I was in the golf course business, I requested a golf cart as my scavenger hunt wish. Despite it being on the list, I never thought they would hijack a golf cart from a nearby golf course. I was incorrect and we ended up hiding the golf cart in the frat house.

The next day, the police came by. Being the vice president of all of the frats, I knew the police well. We were frequently getting reprimanded.

"Bet you guys are here about the golf cart," I said. "It's definitely not here though."

I told him that it was over at Kingston Pizza. The pizza

place was 500 to 600 yards away from the Quadrangle, which was 500 feet in the other direction. The next day, we managed to move it to the Quad and phoned in a call that we had heard someone come back from class and say that it was there. We didn't get caught. It was just some good, clean, relatively harmless fun.

Ram beer

The athletic director, Moe Zachern, was a member of the Quidnessett Country Club where I caddied at the time. Our school mascot was the Rhody Ram. I asked Moe if we could build a big ram, made in the University of Rhode Island's colors and bring it into the game. Moe said sure thing. He was a good sport.

We built an 8 foot tall, 4 to 5 foot wide, 6 foot long ram. Out of the ram's mouth, however, was a beer tap. We didn't tell anyone, because it was illegal and you had to buy beer inside the grounds of the athletic field.

Word got out that the ram was spilling beer, so we had to remove it from the football field. We never saw the second half of the football game, but we brought the ram home and the beer kept flowing, so it was all good.

Those were the kinds of things we did, but we didn't get in trouble.

Building bar beer collection

The brothers wanted a new bar, so they challenged us to build a bar that wouldn't cost any money to build.

I managed to find this old farmhouse and it had a fabulous old barn wood. It was fantastic. We got all the wood we needed from there. Over years, we had amassed a tremendous beer collection that also needed a beer case.

I'm not too proud of this next part, but since the statute of limitations has lapsed, we managed to obtain additional materials from the fine arts building on campus. All the artwork, sculptures and paintings were enclosed in plexiglass to display the artwork. We decided to do remove the plexiglass and use it to build out a beer case. Because the security wasn't much at all then, we unscrewed the plexiglass and took it out. By repurposing the plexiglass it didn't cost us a penny and it came out pretty good.

Bathroom stalls

We used to study in this hall, Independence Hall, which was right across from the fraternity. Our frat house was always very loud with people coming in and out. We also didn't have quiet hours. In going to Independence Hall, we got to know the janitors, who left the building by 9 p.m. and worked Monday through Thursday.

One of our bathrooms at the frat house had no separating partitions between the toilets. One other fact about those campus janitors was the fact that they never locked the doors at the end of their shifts. One Thursday during my junior year after the janitors had bid us adieu for the weekend, we went to the second floor of Independence Hall and decided to take apart the stalls that were in the bathroom and bring them across the street to the fraternity. We had a secret room where we could hide them and painted them in totally different colors and no one knew.

We had rehearsed a plan of what to say, so when the janitors returned on Monday, we asked: "are you guys trying to redo the bathrooms? There are no stalls in here."

Sal of Phi Mu Delta

Phi Mu Delta was comprised of mostly athletic individuals, many of which were on the football team. On and off through the years, the fraternity was put on probation. We'd invite them over to our fraternity on Thursday nights along with a couple sororities. One night, I walked into the kitchen and there was this very big guy named Sal, who was picking a fight. He was very drunk and happened to have a meat cleaver in his hand. He had been chugging beer and was slugging shots of peppermint schnapps. I don't know what came over me, but I went right up to him and suggested that he put down the cleaver and leave.

People around me were stunned. But that's what he did. He put down the weapon and left.

To this day, I have no idea what I was thinking, but that's what happened that night in the kitchen.

Blizzard '78

Our rooms in the frat house were basically a place to store your clothes. We only had 14 rooms, so there was a lot doubling up in these rooms in bunk beds. We all slept upstairs, where there was no heat or outlets to use electricity. We slept that way for all four years that I attended the University of Rhode Island.

For those that snored, well, you'd best beware, because if you did, you were the recipient of a steady stream of flying boots. People would pick them up and chuck them. Sometimes, their sleeping neighbors would get hit. We also slept with the windows open.

In 1978, there was a big snowstorm. This is one of those things you can't believe. We were going back to the URI the night of the blizzard. I still remember talking to my friend Ernie and there was no one on the road.

When the blizzard hit, and the power went out and we

couldn't find our beds, all 40 of us were crowded around in sleeping bags. We just told stories. I was so fortunate because we had such a mix of people -- we had scholars, alcoholics and people in-between -- it was such a great mix.

I still remember the snow coming in the windows. I don't think you can get away living like that nowadays.

The Volkswagen Beetle

I never smoked pot in college, but I knew how to grow it. The SAE frat was next door. Their brothers were bartenders at The Union and were smokers. I asked them if they could give me some seeds and I told them I may be able to grow some weed for them.

I had a Volkswagen Beetle at the time and I drove to the place where we could throw some seeds at the backside of the dump near the golf course where no one could see what was happening. As it turns out, they grew extremely well.

When they got to a certain height, I put them in seven black trash bags and drove them over to the university. I told 'em: "I've got a bag of pot for you guys."

The fraternity had all these secret rooms that provided us an opportunity to dry out the pot plants. Some claimed I was a drug dealer, but I think I was just putting science to good use. I drank free for a whole year by helping out those bartenders. It was great.

The following year one of my frat brothers planted some of the crops in the middle of nowhere in the woods that was surrounded by a stone wall and gate out front. Their thinking was to prevent the critters from getting in.

The week before it was time to harvest, someone harvested it for them. They thought I had, but to this day, I have no idea who it was.

Peter and the clock

Peter Wells was one of my fraternity brothers. He was pretty clever and creative. He sent pledges to the house of the president of the university. Peter and his boys went over and sang the University of Rhode Island theme song to the president. One night during a song, Peter decided to take the president's clock off of the mantle and take it back to our fraternity house as proof.

A week or so later, we returned the clock and told the president what had happened. He was a good guy. Very often we'd sing to him, because the pub was right below where he lived.

Back then we could get into that kind of mischief and get away with it.

Peter went on to become a very successful architect.

Staying in touch

In order to become a brother of our fraternity, you went through quite a bit of hazing. Our hazing was pretty intense -- we had no sleep for a week.

We also needed to keep a goldfish alive for a week. No matter where you went, you had to have your goldfish with you. If you didn't, you were reprimanded. As part of the challenge, we put 600 goldfish in Ziploc bags all over the house.

I can remember my senior year talking to a freshman, who said, "If I don't leave here, this place will kill me." It's reality. You have to move on.

As hard as that was, we all knew we had to do it. We had about six or seven brothers in my class, that told everyone they were on the five-year plan. After we graduated, we wanted to continue our fun and made an agreement to keep in touch. Following our graduation, we went to Times Square on New Year's Eve and attended Mardi Gras. Following Mardi Gras, we went to Scarborough Beach where he had an a-frame house on the water. We were drinking and playing games, while the ocean got fierce and waves were crashing across the sliding doors. Rather than evacuate the house, the twenty of us decided to sleep on a higher floor in the house. Not the smartest decision we made but it seemed sensible in the state we were in at the time. We also connected in Clinton, MA to celebrate St. Patrick's Day. Six months later we met to do something physically crazy and that's where my first marathon ensued. A lot of us had moved away, but we still followed through with our plans.

Greek Life, Pudgy and Big Ass Dot
Dennis Gagne

In the early 1970's, Greek life was a lot of fun and full of shenanigans. When you think about 40 or so young men living under one roof, there are bound to be some personality differences and many guys who are frequently up to hijinks. One brother from my pledge year was sort of a loner. He seldom got involved in house social activities other than intramural sports. His nickname was Pudgy, though he wasn't fat but actually rather fit. We called him Pudgy just to piss him off.

Often fraternities played friendly tricks on sororities with most of it being harmless and playful. However, one such trick included stealing trophies and it had escalated into a series of back and forth raids including theft of composite photos and even dumping bags of dirt into the spotless sorority house. The retaliation by the women was epic and led to a very funny incident that fortunately didn't lead to any real harm.

Pudgy was a good student and often woke up very early to study while the fraternity house was quiet. One morning, he was delighted to find a plate of chocolate chip cookies in the social room, just inside the front door of the house. As he studied in solitude, he munched away at the cookies. Some brothers found remnants of the delights but didn't think much about it with the exception of inquiring why there were no more cookies. Pudgy had gone off to morning classes and returned shortly before lunch. Most of us ate together at 12:30 along with members who lived "down the line" or in off campus so the dining room was full along with house-mother at the head table.

We had a cook who we referred to as "Big Ass Dot" or "Dirty Dot". She was quite plump and could be VERY ornery. Never piss Dot kitchen' while wielding a spatula. Pudgy ran into the adjacent game room and finished his business in another trash can, because he could never have made it up two flights of stairs to the head. Needless to say, we knew who ate the cookies. A few of the brothers who were dating women from the sorority had tipped them off that the chocolate chips in the cookies were actually ex-lax.

Dot was furious and the kitchen had to be thoroughly cleaned with the trash containers thrown out. I don't think Pudgy ever got made-to-order breakfast for the remainder of his time in the house.

Chapter 9
Mom and Dad

As the old saying goes the "Apple doesn't fall far from the tree", and though there may be many subtle differences between my mom, my dad and me, I think it's pretty apparent that we all at the very least come from the same orchard. Not to mention, that both of them would absolutely be considered the "apples of my eye."

Dad

The jade ring

I remember the story of the jade ring like it was yesterday. It was my first real vivid memory of my father. In 1963, while I was in the first grade and living in Texas, my father bought my mother this very expensive and special jade ring. Under today's standards, it might not be considered to be expensive, but everything was expensive to us back then.

We had previously lived in the Philippines and I think that's where my mother first set her sights on jade rings. Ever since, she always wanted one of her own. But due to financial constraints, buying something like that wasn't really an option.

One day, my father got her one. He hadn't wrapped it to that point and somehow dropped it while he was in the back yard. I walked out and saw him in a mild panic, praying on his hands and knees while occasionally crawling around the back yard. He knew that I knew what was going on, but he still felt the need to say, "Bill, sometimes it's good to pray."

I had never seen him get very emotional like that. Moments later, his knee hit the ring and he was immediately overjoyed with emotion.

The power of prayer.

An inconvenience

My father had a unique philosophy about cars and driving. My sisters, Joyce and Nancy, were learning to drive and ultimately got their licenses.

Joyce, who is older, was making a left-hand turn onto Route 1 in North Kingston, RI and got into a crash. She was about a half-a-mile away from home when it happened.

When she got home, she had to face the wrath of my father.

"Dad, it wasn't my fault," she pleaded. "I got hit from behind."

But my father had a different perspective on the matter. He was pretty upset about it.

"If you weren't driving, it (the crash) wouldn't have happened," he said. "It is your fault."

He's right, but he isn't right.

Financially it wasn't a big deal. The car Joyce was driving was my father's and he was merely inconvenienced by having it sent to the garage for a bit. All in all, it was just a small fender-bender.

At least he mellowed a bit since he's gotten older.

Jingles passes

I had a dog for 13 years named, "Jingles." Jingles was a mutt, a bit of this and a bit of that with some beagle sprinkled in. We'd gotten her at Christmastime, so she was aptly named Jingles after Jingle Bells.

In 1973, I was away at college at the University of Rhode Island when my father called me up and suggested I come home. I was planning on coming home anyways, but he urged me to get home quickly because he said my dog was sick.

"Bill, ya gotta come home. Your dog isn't doing so well," he said.

Dad was close to Jingles as well.

When I came home, I headed straight to my bedroom and found my dad sitting beside Jingles on the bed. Dad had this tremendous strength when adversity of any kind would

happen but especially when people or animals were close to passing away. He was always stoic and strong, and always there for his friends. I remember how strong he was with the passing of his own mother who suffered from Alzheimer's disease.

"Bill, come over here, I think Jingles has been waiting for you," he said to me. "She's very sick and I don't think she'll make it much longer."

Five minutes later she passed away. I remember how strong my dad was at that moment. He always seemed to be at his strongest in times when others might find themselves to be weak. I'm strong, but definitely not as strong as him. It's like I'm a respectable .290 hitter, while he's 350.

Fishing for laughs

It was the middle of summer during my junior year of high school when my dad and I rented a canoe and decided to go bass fishing at Gilbert Stuart, a popular fishing spot in North Kingstown, Rhode Island. A canoe isn't exactly the best mode of transport if two people are going to be leaning over the edge at the same time. But when I had a bite, he and I both leaned simultaneously and the canoe flipped. To paint a better picture of the event, my father was especially round at that point and bald, so when we flipped, his head just bobbed up and down in the water like a fishing bobber. It was the funniest thing I've ever seen.

My father couldn't swim very well either, but luckily, we weren't too far from the shore. What capped off the moment is that when he surfaced, the first thing he asked was if I still had the fish. And miraculously I did.

The famous switch

Usually, my father had a very happy-go-lucky disposition, but I saw that change the day of my wedding at Newport Navy Base. We didn't know whether we'd even have a wedding at all as Hurricane Gloria struck and we had to hold our rehearsal dinner by candlelight.

My soon to be bride, Brooke was extremely anal and very precise. The wedding had an Olympic theme and everyone was supposed to carry lighted candles as they entered the chapel.

A young ensign, who held a lower rank than my father, advised us that candles were not allowed in the chapel, and Brooke became quite upset. In response, my father, who was a warrant officer and the person in charge of the chapel, followed the ensign.

"I'll take care of it," he said.

He then cornered the young ensign, poked his pointer finger into the ensign's chest, and said: "Now, you listen here, son. I served in the U.S. Navy for 30 years and I'm a purple heart recipient. I outrank you. I have complete faith that when my future daughter-in-law got permission, she got permission. Let her do what she was allowed to do or else. Do you understand me?"

Needless to say, the ensign backed down and with a slight quiver in his voice, said, "Yes, sir. I understand." My father was very successful in resolving his concern about the candles in the chapel.

Proud of me

Growing up in a military house, it was kind of assumed that you would enter the military too. I always sensed I didn't have my father's respect because I chose not to enlist. When I decided to stay home with the kids, I somehow felt I didn't measure up in his eyes. I thought my father would rather I joined the military like my other family members had as opposed to changing diapers and all the typically feminine stuff like taking kids to school and not fighting for the country.

These thoughts were always on my mind when we'd visit my parents in Rhode Island. When my wife was

traveling one day, I brought the kids down to see my folks by myself. The kids were three and four years old and we had a great day.

My father came up to me and he said, "Ya know what Bill, I'm so proud of you for raising such great kids. It's something I truly missed while being away. I'm very proud of you for what you've done."

That was a huge moment. At times our relationship struggled, because I'd believed he was somewhat disappointed and that he would have been happier if I joined the Navy. I think it put us on equal footing and we got along extremely well from that point on. I'd realized I gained his respect after all. It meant a lot. I was truly blessed to have him say that. It was a good moment.

Amer-I-can

One of my father's frequent pep talks included him encouraging my sisters and I that we could do all things we put our minds to. He always reminded us to think of the word, "American." The last four

111

letters of that word are "I can ." He told us never to forget that. And I haven't to this day.

Mom

Christmas trees

When we were living in Kingsville, Texas around Christmastime, I knew my mom didn't have much money and I got an entrepreneurial streak.

We lived next door to a Christmas tree stand. Even back then, I had an interest in plants and making things with plant materials though I was only in first grade. I thought, geez, maybe I can sell Christmas trees, too.

So, I picked up all the broken branches from the Christmas tree stand and brought them home. I found old cans that previously had contained peas or carrots and I made tiny Christmas trees in those little cans and tried to sell them around the neighborhood.

I gave my mother all the money I raised from selling trees.

"Mom, this is to help with Christmas," I said.

From that time on, my mother and I really bonded. I think it gave us a basis for really close relationship. I have always had a tremendous respect for my mom and it seemed like she had the same for me.

Chocolates, all mine

My mother was a big fan of chocolate. I remember in first grade she had just had surgery, but still suggested we attend the Easter egg hunt because she wanted chocolate so badly.

She took off, as she would say, like a bat outta hell, chasing after the chocolate eggs. I just meandered around at a leisurely pace picking up jellybeans.

Afterwards, I went up to my mother and asked if I could have some of her chocolate eggs because I didn't get any.

"Son, that's your problem," she said.

Whenever chocolate was in the conversation, that's just how she was. She never shared her chocolate with anyone.

Even at her funeral Mass, we gave away chocolate Hershey bars to everyone as a fond remembrance of Mom.

Dad and Mom Pennington at Christmas

My son

When I was a kid, I learned that my mother ran the house. I can remember coming home for school wanting to play. I told her that my friends didn't have to do their homework after school and they could go out to play.

"I don't care about them, I care about my son. When you live in this house, you do what I say," she advised.

She was very consistent with that sentiment up until I was out of the house.

"I know what's best for my son," she'd say.

That's my boy

Out of my two parents, my mother was more of the athlete. She swam a lot, played tennis, and was always watching sports. I played a lot of sports in high school and she was always so proud of what I was doing. I don't think she ever missed a game.

Sitting in the stands at the games, she'd look over to the other parents and say, "that's *my* son." She always emphasized the *"my"* in the sentiment. Even to my dad. It was never "our" son. It was always "my" son.

When Alzheimer's started to set in, she'd still always say, "that's *my* son" or *"my* son is here." She was always extremely proud of me.

Better than the bowling alley

When I was in high school around 1969 around the time of Woodstock, there was a tremendous explosion of drugs in America. Down the street from where we lived there was a bowling alley. There was a tremendous quantity of drugs being sold and bought near there. I didn't go that route because I played a lot of sports.

My mother told me that I could do whatever I wanted to do in the back yard, so I did. I created a huge garden. I had five different varieties of apples and grew roses for my high school girlfriend and mom.

One day I came home and told my mother that I wanted to tear up the back yard. She agreed to it without any reaction. I made a checkerboard of grass comprised of different shades and varieties of grass. When my father came home, there I was with a sod cutter, dump truck and four to five workers.

My mother, who ran the house, told my dad, "Gunner, let him do whatever he wants to the back yard - at least it's better than hanging around at the bowling alley."

When I sold the house after my parents had passed away, you could still see the different varieties of grass that were planted there.

Dedicated to happiness

My father and mother were married for 50 years. For the majority of that time, they had a perfect marriage. They had tremendous respect for each other. Near the end, Dad was more or less confined to a wheelchair at an assisted living facility. Both of them lived there; Dad due to his physical demise and Mom due to Alzheimer's.

They had pretty good safeguards in place and that was important because my mother was constantly encouraging my father to get up out of the wheelchair. Sometimes, her delivery was okay and other times, it was extremely harsh. What she didn't realize was just how difficult it was for him to get out of the chair. She wanted to get out and do things together but his lack of mobility held her back. She would tell him that he was stopping her from doing things that she likes to do.

115

When I became more aware of what it was all about, I realized it was caused by my mother's Alzheimer's. My poor father still had it together mentally. When she'd say something like that, I would tell him that it was the disease talking.

There was one day he got his wheelchair out of the facility and started to let it roll down the steep hill after my mother had encouraged him to get out of the wheelchair again. He wanted to commit suicide. He told me so. He got it going down the hill and it hit a car before he gained too much speed.

He knew exactly what he was saying when he told me, "Bill, I'm making the woman I love miserable, and I don't want to do it anymore. She'd be better off without me," he said.

One of the most awful things we had to do as children was separate my parents. The disease was causing my mother to harass my father. It was really a difficult, yet necessary, decision we had to make for the good of both of them.

Walker

When my mother was suffering from Alzheimer's, we were still trying to get her to physically walk. The trouble was, when she would start to walk, she would also fall. Ultimately, it was recommended she use a walker.

I can remember one of the nurses had a talk with my mother and said, "Mrs. Pennington, due to the fact that you're having some balancing problems, we suggest you use the walker."

When I looked across the room, I saw the look on my mother's face. I've seen that look thousands of times before when she gets upset and I knew that this was not going to end well, so I started walking over to her.

"I'm a Marine. I don't need this," she said as she picked up the walker and chucked it across the room.

I looked up to the heavens and said, "Lord, take her now. I'd be thrilled."

The walker landed and I told the nurse: "Just let her be and let me have that walker. I have an idea."

I went and got a Marine Corps sticker from the Army/Navy store. I ended up getting some note paper off the front desk and came in with this walker. I told my mother that the walker was from the Marines and that there was a letter with it. The letter read:

Cpl. Pennington,

You are required to use this walker three times a day. We want you to march around the facility three times a day.

"Those are your orders", I told her. Upon telling her this, she reacted immediately.

"I have to do this right now," she said.

From that point on until the day she died, she followed those orders.

Each time I'd see her from that moment on, I just prayed that she would act like the mother I knew and grew up with.

Always a Marine

About three or four weeks before she passed away my mother was barely talking. At the most, I would get three or four words per hour -long visit. I would introduce myself. I'd always say, "Hey Mom, Bill's here." I did that so I never had to hear the "who are you?" and thank God I never had to hear that.

If I held up my cellphone by her ear, I would play the Marine Corps Hymn and she would always sing it. Though she was not talking, she would sing the hymn like she was 15 years old.

I would also put the Marine Corps flag in her hand and she would wave it. After she finished singing, I tried to take the flag out of her hand. I didn't want her to poke her eye out or poke my eye out with the flag. When I did try to grab it, she said as clear as can be, "That's my flag." This was the same woman that wasn't speaking.

Eventually she dozed off and I was able to pull the flag out of her tight grip.

Pull up your pants

At my mother's funeral mass, I can remember the packed Lutheran Church that my parents attended in East Greenwich, Rhode Island. The eulogy I gave had a Top 10 list of moments and memories of my mother that included the Easter egg hunt and her not sharing chocolates.

When I got to number 10, I shared something that she said to me whenever I was sad, upset or moping around the house. It was planned, but I didn't think I would be able to pull it off at the mass. She'd say, "Just pull up your fucking pants and act like a Marine."

I said that in church and I didn't get one complaint. Everyone knew.

Even the pastor said, "Bill, that's the spirit of your mom."

Ken Shapiro, my best friend, said, "Only Bill Pennington would get away with that."

And that's my Mom and Dad.

Memories of My Grandma
Sarah Ivey - Bill's Niece

I am incredibly blessed to have so many amazing memories of my Grandma. She was an amazing woman who was kind, hardworking, inspiring, compassionate, and comical. I am so lucky that she was a part of my life well into my twenties. It's very difficult to pick just one special memory, so instead I chose to reflect on a couple of things that bonded us as Grandma and Granddaughter.

I started swimming in fifth grade and as soon as I began, my Grandma supported me right away. She was always so complimentary of how hard I worked as a swimmer. I'll never forget one year when my grandparents came to Georgia for Christmas and watched the end of one of my swim practices. It meant so much to me to have them come watch me swim. Swimming was something that bonded us together for many years.

Probably the most warm and memorable part of our relationship was our mutual love for The Wizard of Oz. In third grade, my class put on the play and it instantly became one of my favorite books. I wasn't aware that Judy Garland was one of my grandma's favorite actresses, and she too was a huge fan of both the movie and the book. Even when Alzheimer's started to impact her life, my grandma was always able to sing songs from The Wizard of Oz with me. The characters were something that never vacated her mind, even when things were difficult. I shared a quote from L. Frank Baum, the author of the book, during my comments at Grandma's funeral, and now I am the proud owner of her Wizard of Oz character plates and her character magnets. I am so thankful that my grandma and I were able to bond over swimming and

The Wizard of Oz over the years. To this day, I hold both memories very close to my heart.

In April of 2016, my then fiancé Joey and I flew to Boston to surprise my uncle, Bill Pennington, at his Run for the Troops event in Andover, Massachusetts. While there, my aunt, Nancy Pennington, took Joey and I to see my grandma at her nursing home. We were not really sure how it would go, but we had a great time. After introducing Joey to Grandma she got very interested in trying to figure out what he was doing there. She kept saying, "So Jose, what is your role here?" Needless to say it made all of us laugh. Although I don't know if she realized he was my future husband that she was meeting, it meant so much to me that she was able to connect with Joey. A year after we got married, we were able to see her one more time. I have a vivid memory of Joey pushing her down the hall in her wheelchair. We are both so glad that we had the opportunity to make such special memories with Grandma.

Memories of My Grandpa
Sarah Ivey - Bill's Niece

My Grandpa was the funniest person ever. He made light of any situation and could always put a smile on my face. He was a proud Navy veteran and a proud citizen of the greatest country; The United States of America. My Grandpa's sense of patriotism and sense of humor are what I remember the most of about this incredible man.

His hilarious personality would always keep me on my toes. I remember multiple occasions where I would return from swimming laps at the pool or working out at the gym and he would sniff the air and say, "Phew!" After I took a shower, he would say, "Well now that's a little more like it!" These silly comments always made me laugh. When someone would burp at the table he would say, "Bring the rest up at the next meeting and we will vote on it!" This is something that I've carried on with my own family and friends, and it always brings a smile and laugh to everyone!

To say that he was a patriot would be an understatement. He proudly served in the Navy for 30 years. One of my fondest memories was each morning when Grandpa would raise the American flag and each night when he would lower it and fold it very carefully. This was such a small part of his day, but the way he did it was full of honor, love, and respect for his country. He would remind us that you can't spell American without AMER-I-CAN and that because I am an American, I CAN do anything that I set my mind to. Anything is possible because in America, I CAN. To this day, I can remember that he would write it in all capital letters on a napkin. I'm proud to be the Granddaughter of such an amazing patriot

. The April Fool's Joke is on You
Nancy Pennington – Bill's sister

"Once upon a time" is the way mom used to tell bedtime stories to us kids when we were young. So in her honor, I will start my story with the same opening sentence…

Once upon a time there was a man named Gunner and a woman named Chotsie who lived in Rhode Island in a suburban neighborhood. The neighbors who lived across the street from them were very friendly and both families received their newspaper delivery daily. The neighbor's newspaper was thrown into their driveway and Gunner would always take time to walk across the street and put their paper near the garage door so that they could simply raise the garage door and retrieve the newspaper.

On April Fool's Day one year (Gunner's favorite day of the year) Gunner and Chotsie would come up with some clever way to have some fun with the newspaper!

They would work together to not only come up with the idea, but also to execute their plan.

Here are a few tricks they played on their unsuspecting neighbors over the years:

- *They saved a newspaper from a previous date, maybe a few months earlier, and swapped it out for the paper that was delivered on April 1.*

- *They would buy a newspaper that was written in Italian or Portuguese and substitute it for the April 1 newspaper.*

- *They would get the newspaper early in the morning, rearrange the pages and put it back into the plastic bag.*

- *One time they used an old newspaper and shredded it. Then they put it back in the plastic bag making the neighbors think that their newspaper was totally unreadable.*

No matter which of these pranks Gunner and Chotsie decided to do, they would always save the actual newspaper and give it to the neighbors later in the day. What a great sense of humor!!

Joyce, Bill and Nancy at Cadillac Mtn in Bar Harbor, ME

Chapter 10
All The Girls I Loved Before

The saying goes, "Behind every good man is an even better woman". I think this holds true in my life more than any other adage. At the risk of being self-deprecating, I think many who know me would agree with this theory as well.

Tina was my first attempt at dating and became my first serious girlfriend when I was a high school senior and Tina was a year behind me. She had the locker next to mine so it felt like destiny. When you get a signal like adjoining lockers, you know it's meant to be.

Everyone called her name was Clementine, which was her middle name, but I just called her Clem. She and I dated for over a year, until when I graduated and went off to college, while she was stuck back in high school. Clem saw the fraternity life I was living and enjoying and got a little insecure. Though a very positive experience, it didn't last through college. All in all, we got along really well and I enjoyed her family, especially her father and mother. She was a big hit in my family as well. Though short-lived, it was a good positive first dating experience and I will always have fond memories of high school and our prom together.

My next attempt at finding Mrs. Right was pretty interesting as Martha Swanson was someone I knew for quite some time. I played football with her brother and she was like the all American Girl next door. We knew each other in high school, but when we both went off to college we stayed in touch. After college is the time where we became extremely good friends. She and I would run together all the time and hang out. She would help me with events and I was good friends with her family. Martha lived on a farm and was very down to earth.

Everyone in our running community would encourage me. "What goes, Bill? Why don't you guys go out?" I was fine with the arrangement. We were 24-25 years old and I would go to her family's farm occasionally. Her mother and I got along extremely well and I'd go there for dinner. Every once in a while, when we would run, Martha would talk about George a little bit. I never really gave it any serious thought. Just assumed George was another running buddy. Well one night, she was off with George and I was having dinner in Jamestown with her mother, Nancy. In conversation, I hinted, "I think I'm gonna ask your daughter out on a more serious basis." Her mother just kind of smiled at me and didn't say much.

I remember what happened next clear as day even though it was more than forty years ago. We were having dinner upstairs and all of a sudden, I hear Martha running up the stairs. "Guys, you won't believe it. George asked me to marry him." I looked at the mother who was as shocked as I was. And so they got married.

I was happy for her but later asked her about it. I said, "I was thinking of asking you out. How come we never went out?"

She said, "George was stable. You were six or seven years older and you were still the college guy. Doing your college stuff." And she was right.

A few years later, I got married and Martha was actually in my wedding. Both she and my sister were pregnant in the party so they sort of balanced each other out.

To this day, she and I have remained really good friends. One of her daughters and I actually share a birthday. Martha sends me cookies occasionally over the years and we still stay in touch. We tease each other about what could have been.

Martha's got four kids and George has been wonderful; a really good guy. A lot different than I am. He's very solid, easygoing, stay at home guy and I'm happy for that. It worked out.

Next came Debbie. I met her in 1983 while putting on these programs with Martha called Run for Fun. They were summer fun runs all throughout southern Rhode Island. At that time, I enjoyed going to bluegrass and a lot of outdoor concerts. I could never play a musical instrument, but I was interested in the whole bluegrass country scene. While at one event this girl showed up wearing a t-shirt from the Hebron Connecticut bluegrass festival. I had been to that show so she and I started up a conversation. She told me she played the mandolin. We kind of got to know each other and at one of the weekly Run for Fun events we bumped into each other.

She told me she just broke up with her boyfriend and is considering moving back to upstate New York. Debbie kept mentioning this girl Judy as her best friend. I knew of a golf course conference coming up in Rochester, NY and where she was moving was going to be about 20 miles from the event. I suggested staying together while I was in her area. She loved the idea and we spent a couple days up there in her house. As it turned out she and Judy were more than friends. They were very special friends. And the reason she moved back to New York was to be with Judy. She was apparently confused at hat point in her life and never really explained that's why she had broken up with her boyfriend. And so, my streak of unfortunate relationships continued.

Shortly thereafter though my streak was broken and I found true love at last. I was investigating joining a ski house and because and my sister was into cross country skiing and joined a ski house in Killington, VT. And this is how I met my future wife, Brooke.

I was living and working in Rochester but joined the ski house in

Killington, which was about 5 hour drive away. On New Year's Eve, I went up there to see a good friend of mine who was an entertainer at a nearby night club. I decide to go out there for New Year, see my sister and meet some new friends.

Well I was at the ski house and was just lounging on the couch. I think I had sweatpants on or something and in comes this extremely cute. She was with this guy wearing a very fancy shirt, neatly pressed with cuff links. I thought, this must be the girl that my sister, Nancy told me about. This must be Brooke.

I introduced myself and she introduced her friend, Howie, who I assumed at the time was a boyfriend. I went out on my own early on New Year's Eve to go see my friend play happy hour. I told Brooke and my sister, "I'll meet up with you guys later." They told me what bar they were going to. I had a few cocktails listening to my friend, DJ Sullivan, a very funny entertainer.

I had a few cocktails then I went back to the bar where Brooke was with Howie and the rest of the people from the ski house. There was this guy entertaining up there and basically singing by himself. I asked him if he needed any help. He was a good sport and invited me up on stage to join him. We sang a few songs together and then I noticed Brooke was in the front row with Howie. Brooke has very brown eyes, so I suggested, "Why don't we sing Brown Eyed Girl dedicated to Brooke down there."

I think she must have been impressed. About two weeks later, it was my birthday. And once again, I'm on the couch on a Friday night. The weatherman predicted two feet of fresh snow and the conditions were going to be superb. Brooke came in by herself and I turned around and said, "Hey, I'm glad you made it. Where's your buddy?" She said, "I'm glad I made it too. Well, he's not gonna come up to this until the conditions are better."

I was sitting right next to her and I kind of pulled back the curtains. The light was shining in and the snow was coming down like crazy. And I said, "Well, Brooke, I don't think we're talking about the ski conditions, are we?"

She just laughed and we had a fabulous time because Howie wasn't around. She hung out with me because it was my birthday. And right away, we seemed to really hit it off. We went to see DJ Sullivan play and she was a phenomenal skier while I was a maybe an advanced beginner, but I learned very quickly. Brooke was very attractive and would ski anything. If I didn't keep up with her others would.

She loves to ski moguls and while following her, I went up in the air and when I landed, my right ski came off and I landed right on the binding. Believe it or not, I still have the indentation in my muscle. I joked that it is my tattoo for keeping up with her.

Our next date, we actually went whitewater rafting on the Hudson River in early March. I told her I can't really come up for a while, as I needed to train for Boston. She lived in New Jersey at the time in a town called Old Bridge. She was a store manager for Macy's at the time, a high end executive and I'm just growing grass up in RI. I think she really enjoyed change of scenery though. She would put on her jeans when she left New Jersey, would drive up, stay at my house and she loved being on the golf course. She was a pre-med major in college, so she had a kind of a scientific mind and knew what I was saying as I'd talk about plants and why they grow. She was really interested and loved helping out when I'd turn on the water and change cups at the course. I think she really enjoyed the change of pace. Plus she loved the ocean, she loves the workout and was extremely athletic. She thought nothing of biking down to the beach about 20 miles away, spending the day at the beach, and then biking back. All in all, we got along extremely well.

I moved to New Jersey and got a big time job right up the street from where her parents lived. I had a way to go impressing her mother as I was a lot different than the typical guy Brooke would date. They were more used to the coat and tie boyfriend coming over and I would show up in my jeans and my sweatshirt or my running clothes. Her father and I got along extremely well and I think he really enjoyed talking golf.

Brooke was very strong willed, very determined and very capable. Her father wished me all the luck in the world. When I first met him, I overheard the family talking in the kitchen. Her mother asked Brooke, "Is Bill just gonna grow grass or is he gonna get like a real job?"

I knew I had my work cut out for me. At the time I was in charge of 18 of 36 holes at Montclair Country Club, one of the best courses in New Jersey. I took her father up and I showed him all around. He was very impressed. I think we were pretty good there.

Brooke and I got engaged in the fall and we moved to Kansas City. We both loved it there and she was working for Macy's is a buyer for the Midwest division. We bought a house and made many friends there. Everything was going great until on, believe it or not, Christmas Eve, the word leaked out that they are closing down the Midwest division of Macy's and moving everything to Atlanta.

I wanted to stay at a big time job I had landed in Kansas City. I loved it there. So we agreed that I would come down because the only argument I couldn't overcome was when she would say, "Well you don't know about Atlanta until you give it a try." Yet I'm very much aware of the weather in Atlanta. It's very, very hot and I have to work outside. So after a great year in Kansas City where we met many, many friends, we temporarily lived in separate cities. Brooke would come up and she got to know a lot of my friends in Kansas City. We ultimately built a house in Georgia and I ultimately moved down after we got married.

The house was in Lilburn, Georgia, which is right next to Stone Mountain. One of the compromises I managed to pull off was building near Stone Mountain, a huge park where a lot of very serious runners train. It's extremely hilly and was great training.

In the fall of 1986 we got married and there's a couple funny stories about getting married. A lot of friends who attended the wedding in Rhode Island were runners, obviously. I had some connections with people who put on road races and my parents lived in a cul de sac. We actually had our own running race on the morning of the wedding, called Run for the Rings. We had banners and numbers. Brooke wore a bridal costume and I had a tux shirt. All my friends had tuxes and the women that were in the wedding party all had wedding headdresses on. It was a great start to an incredible weekend.

We spent about a year and a half down in Atlanta before we realized that we really wanted to be back in New England. I got offered a job in Watertown, MA and she got a job working for a company called Mass Industries, which made a lot of products for Victoria's Secret. We bought a house in Andover and our first child, Greg was born in January 1, 1990. I stayed home and Melissa was born a year and a half later on October 3, 1991.

We had some wonderful memories of the kids. Greg ultimately took up skiing and did really well while Melissa took up snowboarding. We had many great times at Smuggler's Notch playing bingo and skiing with the kids.

Brooke also loves fishing and we went out to Colorado together. I recall fishing with her on one of these crystal clear lakes. She understood how big trout could get, especially lake trout. I tied a grasshopper onto my hook, rather hurriedly because I saw the biggest trout I've ever seen. I estimate that the thing had to be about 20 pounds. It was enormous. We could see him coming after the grasshopper. Brooke and I were so excited. Unfortunately, I didn't tie the hook very well. He didn't break the line when I set the hook but knot didn't hold up and he got away. I don't know who felt worse me or Brooke.

We went whitewater rafting up in Maine early in September. After spending all summer together and I think her mind was made up. I could tell by the conversations we would have that I was the guy. One of the greatest photographs were these two chairs sitting on a deck that were sitting together and they said, "We'll spend the rest of our lives together."

We got engaged in Jamestown, Rhode Island just before the URI -Brown game. We got engaged in the morning and went up to the game to share the news with everyone at the game.

As the title of the book says, despite the fact we later were divorced, I am blessed with memories. We still remain good friends and are very committed to the well-being of our kids. When I had the heart attack, Brooke understood exactly what was going on due to her pre-med background. She was extremely helpful and committed to my health. She would ask me and ask the doctor questions and was very concerned. And she was always there. And one of the things.

We had already been divorced seven years at that time so it meant the world that she had such a level of concern and empathy. I told her, "Brooke, if you're ever in this situation, I'll be there for you."

I go to divorce groups and support groups and I tell them that our anniversary comes at the end of September and drop off flowers at the house I gave her cards saying thank you for all the great memories. I sign the cards , "Thank you for the some of the best years of my life." The people are amazed that I can do that, but I remind them, she is the mother of my children and we had a lot of great years together.

Following the divorce, Allison and I became such good friends. I was very involved with the PTO and she was and still is the executive assistant for the superintendent of schools. Whenever I would put on PTO events, I would chat with Allison. She was very much into running and I was on the decline of running. She wanted to run the Boston Marathon and at that time, I knew a lot of people and the economy was good. I told her I could get her a number. As a charity runner for Lazarus House, I felt I could raise enough money for both of us. As it turns out, I was able to raise over $7,000 and I gave her the half of mine so she could run the marathon.

We were both involved putting on road races. I was putting on road races in Andover and she was putting them on in Salem. The friendship developed over time. It became more serious years later and she's the one who actually brought me to the hospital when I was ordered to get checked out for the heart attack

We both through health challenges and I was very involved when she learned she had colon cancer stage three. I think the colon cancer was a lot more difficult to not only witness but to go through because of all the chemo and seeing her losing her hair and witnessing the struggles of the impact of chemo. As difficult as that was, I was so glad to be able to support her during those very trying days.

Allison had two daughters, Natalie and Kerry, and I became very close with them and enjoyed being with them. One of my greatest moments with Natalie was when I would follow them and support them on my bike when they would run marathons or road races. Natalie was running the Claire's Dunbar marathon. I have witnessed several marathons where runners were falling apart at mile 17. I telephoned Alison and told her Natalie doesn't look very good at all. I was really getting worried that she may not make it and I would have given her a 10% chance of finishing that marathon. She managed to pull herself together and actually did extremely well. Her guts and stick-to-itness was extremely powerful. I followed her on the bike with all kinds of water, goo and anything she needed. But she did it all by herself.

Her other daughter, Kerry was seriously thinking of going into the army. and is the type that needs to be in charge. She is extremely determined. When she was in ninth grade, she tried out for the cross country team because her mother ran and I think she wanted to be part of that by spending time with her mother. I used to go to the cross country meets and I actually told Allison, "Kerry tries very hard, but man she looks like a newly born colt. I don't think she's ever going to amount to anything as a runner." She worked extremely hard and made herself a great runner. She ultimately qualified for Boston and made the all-state team out of Hamilton–Wenham cross country where she became captain of the cross country team and got a scholarship from Merrimack College for running. She was one of the most fiercely determined individuals I've ever met. And both of them are just great. I think they had a tremendous role model of perseverance and independence in Allison. I'm very blessed to have as many years as I did with them.

Allison was a tremendous football fan. She and I are actually in these football pools and she actually has won the overall pool for the year frequently wins money betting on football games. She is a huge Patriots fan and we actually went down to see the Patriots practice a few times together.

On one of our first dates we went to a Red Sox game. I had really good seats and brought a man who happened to be a priest. She thought that was something I had pulled off but I actually knew this priest. She'd tease me, "You kind of rushed it in the beginning showing up with a priest like he was going to marry us."

Allison was a die-hard Democrat, and I'm not. I'm out to dinner with some Democrats and I'm pretty knowledgeable on the weather and one of them mentioned that the storms were coming in. I said, "Nah, it's not gonna rain." We were sitting outside at a restaurant and I said, "I'll tell you what. If it rains, and we get wet, I'll register as a Democrat." Well, as they say, God is gonna take care of that. And if I wasn't confident, I never would have made the bet. But about 20 minutes later, we had to go inside because it was pouring rain. I actually followed through and registered as a Democrat. They said, "well, you have to vote." I did. I voted in the primary and immediately switched back to independent.

One of the greatest moments of our friendship was when she recovered from colon cancer. She was determined to come all the way back. She ran this marathon that Kerry and I followed on bicycles with her dog. Allison ran the entire 26 miles and in a very good time, a year after being diagnosed with stage three colon cancer. That was probably one of the more impressive things I'd ever witnessed, but that was her goal and her motivation. That's what got her through.

I usually don't get too upset with people, but when she was just starting the chemotherapy and was really feeling down in the dumps, she said, "Bill, I just don't know if I can do this." A little switch went off and I began to lecture her, "Let me understand this. You don't really care about your daughter's. You don't really care about your mother and father. You don't really care that all your friends will miss you. If you don't fight this, you don't care about us and you don't even care about the person talking to you right now." I think that tongue lashing give her a reason to live and a reason to fight. Because when you're facing weeks of chemo, and you question why I am going through this, I think you need to refrain from thinking about you but instead about others and the impact you would have them if you are gone. It was a difficult thing to watch someone you love and support going through cancer but like I said, it was one of the proudest moments when she was diagnosed as cancer free and the smile on her face meant the world.

The year before she got cancer, we were supposed to go the Kentucky Derby. Her daughter, Natalie was going to get a special award, so she postponed it, she could be home to see her receive the award. The following years, we were supposed to go again, but she got diagnosed with cancer. Her goal was to get through the chemo, and then go down to Austin, Texas. I agreed to go as long as I could go to the Broken Spoke, one of the most famous country lesson bars in the world. She said, "Okay, we'll go there on Sunday." I swear that this day, she knew that the Broken Spoke is open Monday through Saturday. When we arrived in the parking lot on Sunday, she smirked and said, "Hey, it looks kind of empty." Unfortunately, it wasn't open. But, we had a great relationship and many years of blessings.

Chapter 11
My Children Growing Up

Among all the special memories that have filled my life, there are no memories as sweet as the indelible moments spent with my two children, Greg and Melissa. The two are the ties that will ever bind, their mother Brooke and me together. The sense of pride that fills me up when I think about the joy these two incredible human beings have brought to us both is beyond description. Without them, I am a shell of the man I am.

Greg

On December 27, 1999, Brooke and I went to the doctors and they said it would be at least a week before baby Greg arrived.

I went to bed on the evening of the 31st, with the plan to do a long run training for the Boston Marathon. However, Brooke woke me up about 4:00 a.m. and informed me that the baby was coming and we ought to assemble the crib. I started to put the crib together and it became immediately evident that we needed to go to the hospital.

"Brooke," I said. "I think we have to go to the hospital and get our priorities in order. The crib will be ready when Greg comes home. I guarantee that. Let's get you to the hospital."

We got in the car and headed to Brigham & Women's where she immediately went into labor. After the thirteenth hour of labor, they were going to give her an epidural. Brooke was a pre-med student, so she knows medical stuff and she was extremely well-prepared with the delivery.

"I understand about the epidural, but how long will it last?" Brooke asked the doctor.

"Did you attend childbirth classes?" the doctor bounced back exhibiting extremely poor bedside manner.

At that point, I thought Brooke was going to jump out of the bed. I intercepted and asked the doctor again if he could tell us how long the epidural would last.

"She's having contractions now and, in some discomfort, so if you could let her know, I'm sure it could offer her some comfort," I said.

Greg was born at 8:58 p.m. through a C-section. The first words out of her mouth when I could finally see Greg and hold him were, "Does he have everything?"

I said, "Yup. He's got his fingers and toes, he looks great. God bless you."

It kind of struck me that she was concerned that he was all right. A caring mother right from the very onset of motherhood.

After Greg was born, I entered a drawing for four tickets to the Masters for the Golf Superintendents Show in January. I was informed the first week of March that I had indeed won four tickets to the king of all golf events. Brooke was already scheduled for a trip for that time period so I stayed home with Greg.

I informed Greg a few years later when we were watching it together that I didn't go to the Masters, so that I could stay home with him. When I told my fellow golf course superintendents about that, they asked how I could do that.

I replied, "When you love your son more than the golf, it's not that hard."

Burning fingers

Greg was about one-year-and-a-half-old when he started reaching toward the gas stove. I'd always tell him, "No. Hot." I don't think there's a child that age that would understand what "hot" actually means. So, being home by myself, I figured I would show him what hot is. I turned on the stove and picked him like a football and put his hand above the flame.

"Greg. Hot. No," I said.

I think he got it especially when I turned the knobs off and the plates remained hot. I went to turn and he stuck his hand on the plate and blistered up his hand. When I took him to the pediatrician, thank goodness I had a good relationship with Dr. Nelken.

"Bill, if I didn't know you, this could be child abuse," the doctor said. "But I believe you and your story and this should be all cleared up by the time his mother gets home."

I think this story will be news to Brooke when she reads this as we never told her of the event. It's not news to Greg however and it was extremely effective because he never touched the stove again.

Toilet paper

When Greg was about three years old and was on the upstairs potty, he told me that he was all set. I told him that I was going to go take out the trash while he did his business. The bathroom was on the second floor and about 16 steps to the bottom floor. I took the garbage cans out the front door and wheeled them up against the street in front of our place. It probably took me about a minute and a half. In that 90 seconds, Greg thought it would be really funny if he took an enormous amount of toilet paper, including the cardboard roll and tried to flush it.

That resulted in the toilet backing up and flooding down the stairs. He was upstairs laughing and giggling, so I headed to the kitchen and stood in front of the sink. The bathroom is located directly above the sink and water was dripping down from the ceiling.

"Okay, Brooke will be home when?" I asked myself.

Greg was having such a good time, how could I yell at him? I thought it was pretty funny, too. Once again, the benefit of Brooke traveling, all I did was paint the ceiling and cover it all up.

This is another one that Brooke may not know about until she reads this.

Stay outside

Greg had to know where I was at all times. He would have to be able to reach out and touch me or he'd get extremely nervous. I was always trying to inspire some independence. When he was about three or four years old, I figured that because we had a fenced-in backyard, he could play in the backyard. What we discovered is that he wouldn't do it without me there. So I decided to force the issue.

I put him outside to play and locked the screen door, so I could make dinner and told him to stay outside.

"It'll be alright," I told him.

He could physically see me, but he couldn't get in through the screen door, which in turn caused him to start crying and get upset. It was unusual for me to push this, but I was determined to get my point across. When he started to throw up out of immense anxiety, I figured that was far enough and I let him come back in.

Even to this day, he really gets nervous. He always wants to know and doesn't do well with the unexpected.

Shrinkage

We had a very big house, but when you're home all day with the kids, the house can get rather small. The kids at this time were probably in third and fourth grade. I told them we had to get outside and I was pretty serious about it.

"Guys, we have to get outside," I told them. "The house is shrinking. It's getting small."

It was February and the floodlights were on, so we went playing out in the snow and having a good time. Brooke came home and Greg went running up to his mother.

"Mommy, Mommy! You can't go in!" he said. "The house is shrinking. We can't go inside."

Not your work

When Greg was in fourth grade, he was blessed with the best teacher he's probably ever had: Mrs. Seavy at South Street Elementary School in Andover. Greg loved the class and knew her from the second day of school. The class had a writing assignment and turned it in quickly and went out to recess. Greg loved this teacher and insisted on sitting in the front row every day. He loved the class and everything about it.

Mrs. Seavey was quite a unique teacher and had her own personal style. She was in high demand with so many of the parents and here's one of the reasons: she held up Greg's paper. In front of the whole class, she says, "I'm a little confused. This paper says it's produced by Greg Pennington and written by Greg Pennington, but I know Greg can do so much better than what's produced on this paper that I don't think it's his paper."

She encouraged Greg to take a better look at it. Greg embraced that kind of feedback. To this day, Mrs. Seavey is still his favorite teacher. She was extremely good with him and challenged him.

Home run

When Greg was in fifth grade and playing Little League, one of his rivals was pitching for one of the better teams in the league at the time. The coach for the other team was strong-willed and very vocal. His son was a pretty good pitcher. While Greg was up at bat, the first pitch was hit foul - it might have been close though. Roger Pierce, the coach and father of the pitcher, called a foul without a doubt. The second one was clearly fair in my eyes and Greg's dad, Roger called it foul again. Both of them would have been home runs had they not been called foul. The third one is probably one of my proudest moments of my son. He hit it between right field and center field, and clearly a home run. As he rounded the bases, he said to Roger, "Are you going to call that foul, too?"

For a fifth-grader to stand up and give some good feedback to the coach was pretty impressive and made me very proud.

Gettysburg Address Pickett's Charge

Greg went to Gettysburg College. During his first year, he got really sick. He also struggled adjusting to college life. He had some roommates that were not the best fit. He did join a fraternity and made some friends though. By the time he was a senior, he was very comfortable and enjoyed the whole college experience. I thought back to how far he came. For someone to adapt and not give up, and press on, I was pretty impressed.

I had been to Gettysburg a few times. I wanted to do something a little different on our visit. And the first thing that kids do when they're freshmen is to get up by the Gettysburg cemetery and recite the Gettysburg Address. I laminated the Gettysburg Address for everyone. I walked up Pickett's Charge and told them the story about it. The Confederates never gave up, I told them. Despite the fact that many of their soldiers were getting killed right in front of them, they didn't give up. I said, "Greg continued to press on. And here we are, Greg has reached the top after four years, despite the struggle."

I had everyone read the Gettysburg Address for Greg.

Despite the fact that Greg doesn't share his emotions very often, he came over to me afterwards and said, "Dad, you made my weekend. Thank you so much."

'I learned it from you'

Greg's birthday is January 1st. Two Christmases ago, I was in the driveway of the house and he and I were chatting about what we're going to do for the next few days while he was here. And he said, "I'm going to New York and staying here and there and there."

"Greg, for you to pull this off, and you have friends all around the world and you can stay with, says an awful lot about you. And you

must have really invested in your friends to be able to do this," I said. "And I'm really proud of you."

You wonder sometimes when you're a stay-at-home dad if it's really worth it. You give up a lot of work career-wise and you're changing diapers. But in that moment, in that driveway, I knew it was worth it because he said: "Dad, I learned it all from you."

142

Melissa

Melissa was born by a C-section delivery at 2:12 p.m. on Oct. 3, 1991. Her delivery was delayed, because ahead of Brooke in line was a mother trying to deliver twins and then another with triplets.

When it was finally Brooke's turn, doctors yelled that they needed help getting her out. I don't know how doctors and mothers do it, but when I heard the doctors yell that they needed a crowbar, I thought they were joking! But then I see them walking back with a piece of equipment that looks exactly like a crowbar and they used it to pry Melissa out. Everything was ultimately fine.

Broken arm

When Melissa was about 3 ½, she liked to jump off of things. While I was making dinner one night, I saw her jumping up and down near this little table that we had that was about two or three feet high. All of a sudden, I hear this sound of her falling to the ground.

I look over at her and say, "Melissa, are you okay?"

And she says, "Yeah, I think so. No big deal."

We continued to have dinner and there's no issue.

About one week later, I tried to touch her arm and she informed me that her arm hurts when it's touched.

"Daddy, it's been hurting me for a while," she said.

"How bad does it hurt?" I said.

"Well, really bad," she said.

Well, I decided to bring her to Dr. Robert Nelken to get her checked out. He performed an X-ray. As it turns out, her arm was broken and the doctor said again, "If I didn't know you … we'd be looking at a problem here," he said. "This child had a broken arm for a week."

Melissa still remembers that pretty well.

Stitches

About one year-and-a-half later, there was a merry-go-round at the playground that I had taken Melissa to. She tells me that I'm pushing too hard and she falls and hits her forehead and it starts bleeding badly. The cut looked pretty bad. Melissa, however, never cries.

I ended up taking her to Andover Pediatrics to see Dr. Nelken and he shot her up with Novocain because he had to put stitches in. Again, she hasn't cried yet.

The doctor goes to put the needle in her forehead and she looks at him as if it were nothing. Even after the stitches, nothing.

"Bill, I've never seen anything like this in all my years at my practice," said Dr. Nelken.

He reiterated again that he had never seen a child react or not react in this manner.

Lawn mower

When Melissa was 9 years old, she got her first concussion, thanks to dad. I was teaching her how to use the lawn mower, which had a pull cord. When you pull the cord, your elbow goes straight back. When you do this, you should have your daughter or whomever stand in front of you rather than behind, so you don't risk an elbow going flying to the forehead. I didn't do that and ended up hitting Melissa in the forehead.

"Are you alright?" I asked.

And she says, "Yeah, I'll be alright."

Melissa finished cutting the lawn and came in to tell me that she doesn't feel right. She says that she has a headache.

As time passed, she kept noting that it was getting worse.

When Brooke came home, we decided to take Melissa to the doctor's office. And most likely, she had her first concussion, due to dad.

Just in case

On Melissa's first day of kindergarten, she sat next to a boy named Jimmy in Connie Barber's class. Jimmy had too many Cheerios or chocolate milk to drink that morning. For most, this may sound like too much to stomach, but not my daughter, who survived stitches and a concussion. Ultimately, little Jimmy threw up right next to Melissa. He didn't get her, but for the rest of the year, I had to be in the kindergarten lobby because Melissa worried that it would happen again. Melissa thinks I must have been there all day instead of just at pick up time, standing guard in case Jimmy threw up again.

School bus

One of the benefits of being home with your kids every day is that you have the opportunity to take them to school, and Melissa knew no different. When Greg was in high school, he took the bus. But not my daughter. When she started playing sports and was on a school bus, she goes, "Oh, this is a school bus? I've never been on a school bus."

Melissa has never ridden on a school bus to school because she had her own private bus driver in Dad. It was kind of a unique experience.

Kicking off ski boot

When Melissa was still in diapers, Greg and I were skiing, along

145

with Brooke, and we decided to teach Melissa how to ski at her relatively young age. Daddy was in charge of teaching Melissa how to ski. She didn't like the ski boots. She told me that they were uncomfortable, didn't fit properly and she was rather upset. We practiced walking around in them, but she still wasn't especially keen on them.

"I think she'll get used to them," I said to my wife. "She'll be fine."

We when headed for the chair lift and we got pull No. 10 at Smuggler's Notch in Vermont. We've been back several times since this incident. Melissa goes nuts. She starts kicking her feet and screaming.

"Daddy! I'm not going to go skiing!" she wailed. "I hate these boots! I HATE these boots!"

I tried to reassure her that everything would be okay, but before I knew it, the boot and the ski came off, falling 30 to 40 feet down to the ground.

As we came to our spot to slide off, I scooped up my daughter and skied down to pick up her boot and ski.

"Melissa, I think it's time for a hot chocolate," I said to her.
"Absolutely, Daddy! Heck with that skiing stuff," she said.

"How about we try snowboarding?" I suggested. "The snow boots for that are actually really comfortable."

By the time Brooke and Greg returned, Melissa was now snowboarding, much to the displeasure of my wife. Melissa wanted to be a little different. It turned out to be a real good thing. One of Melissa's first jobs out of college was teaching snowboarding to inner-city kids out in Boston. Melissa is still an avid snowboarder, thanks to dad.

Bottle of memories

I used to take Melissa and her soccer teams to tournaments. We played in one in Rhode Island and had a grand ol' time. This was probably the first really big tournament these seventh-graders had ever been in.

The night before the tournament, we were out racing go-karts until about 10 o'clock at night. They had a great time, making memories on the beach, getting tattoos and racing go-karts. It's not about winning as much as having a memorable time.

We were in the finals though and they had a 9 a.m. game, so at least they got six hours of sleep before the big game. There were big time spectators coming in the morning to watch the girls play and we needed them to be at their best.

The game arrived and the girls were a bit wound tight. I was trying to figure how to get them to calm down and focus on something other than the game. I went to have a sip of water from my water bottle and bingo! I got it. I went out and purchased 14 little Poland Spring water bottles and passed them out to the team.

I explained to the team, "The water in these bottles represents memories from this weekend. We have a major problem though. When we win this game, we won't have any more room. The bottles are full from memories of this weekend," I told them. "I want you all to take a sip from the top and take memories, so when we win this game, we can put more water in here and that will represent us winning this game."

Of course, we won. To this day, it has become a family tradition. When we go on trips or special things, I give my kids an empty water bottle and instruct them to fill them with memories.

The value of participation

Growing up, Melissa had six concussions. Among those incidents, she got one from her dad, one from snowboarding and once she hit her head in soccer really badly. When she went to college, she couldn't read as a result of the concussions. It would give her severe headaches. She ended up listening to books on tape.

I was visiting in September of her sophomore year and she was doing all of these activities so well. She was handling life much better than she ever had before and seemed willing to engage and take part in so many things. She was doing extremely well in school at Roger Williams.

I had read somewhere once before that when you get concussed, your brain acts differently. Sometimes, people become more intelligent or think differently.

"Melissa, you seem to be doing so much more than you ever have before. What's the deal? What's the story?" I asked.

She and I are very close. I can have these discussions with her.

"Dad, I've missed so much," she said. "I don't want to miss anything."

In high school, she couldn't go out because she was concussed. She'd get headaches if there was too much noise. She understands the value of life and doesn't want to miss out on anything.

How far you've come

Melissa got promoted after one year at the Sarah Holbrook Foundation in Vermont. It's an after-school program for new immigrants. Her role for the up until June, was as a teacher. She would help facilitate the programs. She's starting to do other things like writing grants and reach out beyond her job description on her own. She's even dabbled in marketing.

In recent months, a position opened up as an assistant principal at the school. She asked me if I thought she should apply and I told her to go for it. I thought it would show initiative.

"Dad, I don't think I'm qualified," she said to me.

"You've done some great things, so I say you take a swing and go for it," I said.

Following the interview, she told me that she didn't think she did that well. She said that she was confused by the questions that were asked.

The next day, she called up and told me that she got the job.

"It's not that you got the job, because that's not the big thing," I said. "The big thing is look how far you've come. Where were you ten years ago? Ten years ago, you couldn't read a book. That speaks volumes."

Coincidentally, as I write this book and brag a bit about my daughter, the following email came across my screen. As a boastful and proud father it reads as follows:

"Dad,

I have been selected by the National Afterschool Association as 2021 Next Generation Leader! Hundreds of nominees and I am 1 of 40 to be selected across the country. Christine and a VT after school school -member nominated me. I'm so excited! –Melissa"

This makes me so proud because I know how far she has come. From a young woman who had challenges reading due to multiple concussions to the Next Generation Leader. I don't think I have to tell you, how I'm bursting with pride at the moment.

The note from Melissa was accompanied by an email from the woman who nominated her advising her of her selection as well as the nomination itself.

Congratulations, Melissa,

You have been selected as one of NAA's 2021 Next Generation of Afterschool Leaders! Your work is valued. You deserve to be recognized. NAA is committed to honoring you and supporting your ongoing professional development. You, our next generation of leaders, are crucial to the sustainability, growth, and success of this important

profession!

When I started in my role as ED at Sara Holbrook Community Center, Melissa was the Director of our Elementary Afterschool Program. It was clear from my first meeting with her that she had an amazing ability to understand the big picture of our work, to think strategically, and always with the best interest of our students at heart. Melissa is always looking for ways to increase the quality of our programs and to grow professionally.

In July, Melissa became the Associate Director of the organization, and now oversees our Program Directors and drives the vision for the programs provided by the center. In spite of having never held a position at this level, she has flourished. Since taking on her new role, we have moved our organization, added a toddler program, gone from half to full day in our pre-k program, almost tripled our elementary afterschool program, rebooted our teen programs, AND pivoted to providing support for remote learning by expanding our elementary, middle and high school afterschool programs to a full day.

I have watched Melissa settle into her role as a leader, seamlessly addressing staff and program challenges, setting a tone that is positive, strengths-based, and always focused on growth and development for our students, staff, programs, and herself. She elicits the accolades of other leaders in the field. Not a week goes by that I don't hear from a member of our board, another Executive Director in the community, a leader in the Afterschool world about one interaction or another that they have had with Melissa and how adept she is in her role and how committed she is to youth and third space learning. Our organization is better for her presence and I am grateful to have the opportunity to work with her.

PROUD DAD and with good reason!

The Good Times Shine Through
Brooke Pennington

Life with the kids was always fun. They agreeably went along with most things from chores to adventures and seemed to enjoy all our time together.

It is the times together in regular daily life that were filled with joy, lively spirit and the challenges of growing up that made it wonderful .....from time at home, bedtime stories and all the playtime in the back yard....T-ball, kick ball, baseball, The Citgo sign, tubing runs and being chased by the dogs, skating and playing hockey, lots of birthday parties...to so many places we enjoyed.

Hopefully they feel the love, support, respect and opportunities that surround them, then and now. This has helped make them inspiring people.

As far as stories from the early days:

Melissa's unknown broken arm – an early indication of her

151

endurance.

Greg's squealing excitement for planes and trains - makes him a global influencer now.

Greg randomly picking up a newspaper at age two and reading it!

Both really supporting each other, attending each other's games, recitals, events, cheering each other on and rarely complaining.

Two people who truly understand the importance of taking care of others.

Greg's gentle care for his "little sister" .

There are silly stories that happened, as I am sure happen in all families growing up, but I think these should only be spoken about by the kids, as they may prefer to leave them in their private past. Hope this is helpful and the book is coming together well. It's nice to remember and it's true, the good times shine through.

Brooke Pennington
Bill's ex-wife

Greg and Dad at Fenway

Fishing with Melissa in Lake Eufaula, Alabama

Chapter 12
My Book Wouldn't Be Complete Without...

Tom Dowling

Tom Dowling was such a special friend to so many people I wanted him to have his own story. He owned a health and fitness club called Health Plus in Kansas City, KS. Tom grew up in New Hampshire and was a very successful coach of the cross country team in Laconia, New Hampshire. He had this way of motivating people. I remember when he asked the team how long the basketball and football team practices each day. Members of the team responded by saying they practiced for two to three hours. Tom would say, "There's no difference with running."

People would previously run one hour at most before Tom took the helm. But Tom would have his team work out two to three hours before and after school.

The school was close to Lake Winnipesaukee and somehow, Tom convinced these high school kids to trek the 87 miles around the lake. During the month of February, each member of the cross country team ran the entire 87 miles around the lake. I'm not sure what the temperature was, but it couldn't have been warm. That's the kind of influence and enthusiasm he had for running.

Join me

One day in 1983 , Tom invited me to join him running with his running team. I had no idea how many people were going to show up, but somehow, Tom managed to get 30 people to join us.

I told him that I usually do 22 miles and he said to me, "Well, that's your problem. You're not going long enough."

I was 28 years old at the time, running these gravel roads south of Kansas City. I had no idea how far we were running. I remember at one point, I leaned over and said, "Tommy, how far have we gone?" He just kept looking ahead and told me 18 miles. I couldn't believe we had run that far. It was so easy running with him and that group of people. We stopped at a convenience store around mile 20 where we had our own private bank account of change accumulated from previous runs. We'd leave our spare change and had a running account to pull from as needed.

From there, it was six miles back to Health Plus. That jaunt inspired me to run between 26 and 32 miles every Sunday. We'd all tell jokes, share great stories and became lifelong friends.

Tom always had a bunch of women running alongside him who had iron deficiencies. He encouraged us all to keep our iron levels up. We'd have liver and onions and orange juice after we ran 26 to 32 miles topped with a massive

amount of BBQ sauce.

He also believed that if you ran greater than three hours the body would produce extra red blood cells and consequently more oxygen. It is a state called mitochondria and would create an effect similar to blood doping, where the extra red blood cells make you more efficient as a runner. We would sometimes actually slow our pace down to extend the run over than three hours so we could experience mitochondria.

We'd call Tom Dowling "Lord," and we were his Disciples when we were out there running. We carried that on for years because people believed everything he said like a herd of sheep.

Tom started to have heart problems that he later discovered was an irregular heartbeat. In January 1998, he sought out the care of a cardiologist. By February, he was running on a treadmill and they were measuring his irregular heartbeat.

'Tom had run the Boston Marathon many times in the past and had planned to run it again, before he died. I managed to snag two medals in 1990 when I ran the Boston Marathon. Upon his passing, his service was held at Johnny Kelley's statue in Newton MA at mile 20 of the Boston Marathon route.

Following his service, I ran up to the peak of Mt. Kearsarge, which was a destination that Tom used to run frequently when he lived in New Hampshire. Tom and his brothers grew up in Warren, New Hampshire, and his brothers still reside there. In memory of Tom, I placed the second medal I had received at the base of a pine tree in Warren. It was a nice homage to such a great friend.

Sharon and Alan Carroll

Sharon and Alan Carroll became very good friends after being a part of the Run for the Troops events. Alan would often say, "I'm just out here to enjoy everything." He would ride along in a vehicle and was just thrilled to be out there. He often took photos of the events for us.

Sharon took care of the financial matters regarding the annual event. Together, they always came together to help, without any hesitation. One of their classic lines was: "If we're not here to help people, then why are we here?"

During the COVID-19 global pandemic, I brought them apple pie. The two of them are really a blessing to me.

Nate Walker

Nate Walker was my boss at the Renaissance Golf Club

in Haverhill, Massachusetts. He was the superintendent of the golf course.

I was leaving work on a Thursday in mid-June. I had just parked my cart and was ready to head home when I heard over the radio that they were having a problem with the irrigation pumps.

"I know how to do that, Nate", I said to Nate Walker, the long-time course superintendent at Renaissance Country Club in Haverhill, MA.

"How did you know about the pump issue", Nate asked.

"I heard it on the radio."

Nate said, "But weren't you going home?"

"Yes but you're having issues and I know how to fix it."

I told him the solution suggesting we keep the sprinklers on and flood the driving range. This will act as a relief valve until the pump is repaired.

In order to do this we needed to monitor the situation round the clock. I volunteered to work from 3:30 a.m. until 4:00 p.m. for the next few days.

After it was repaired, I sent Nate a thank you note of appreciation for heeding my advice and letting me participate in the solution. It made me feel extremely valuable to the team.

Chance meeting with Ryan

One Thursday evening in late September of this past year, I was leaving Larosa's Restaurant in Andover and headed over to church. I was walking across the intersection and made eye contact with a man in his late thirties. He looked at me and proclaimed that he was a sinner.

I was taken aback for a moment but said, "Well we better get out of the road or we'll both be dead, so let's discuss this once we get to the sidewalk.

I learned his name was Ryan and Ryan again informed me that he had let the Lord down and he is a sinner. I assured him that I am a sinner too but I'm on my way to church so why doesn't he join me.

I learned his name was Ryan and Ryan again informed me that he had let the Lord down and he is a sinner. I assured him that I am a sinner too but I'm on my way to church so why doesn't he join me.

Ryan agreed and as we walked a bit further, someone cut across my path while I was walking. I said, "Damn him."

Ryan snapped back to me, "See you just sinned."

"I told you I was a sinner, Ryan. That's why I'm going to bring you to church with me. I'll introduce to some people, it's right around the corner."

Ryan responded, "Really?"

Upon our arrival, I introduced him to Pastor Mac McSweeney, who works at Lawrence General Hospital and is a member at Free Christian Church.

I told Mac that Ryan is a friend of mine. They hit it off and after church I introduced him to Pastor John Paul and let him spend some time with Ryan.

I followed up with Ryan before I left church and I could tell he was in a desperate place and needed to go to church. He thanked me and his since found a home at Free Christian Church.

Recently I heard he has joined a small group where they discuss bible verses and share stories about where they are in life. He has become more involved.

Many people who I've told the story see our chance meeting as God's will and believe there was a reason we had run into each other.

Chapter 13
Life of Bill Through the Eyes of Others

Bill the Military Man
Joyce Larson – Bill's sister

As a young boy, Bill was fascinated with Army men. He would take these small plastic figures and arrange them as if they were preparing for battle. He had hundreds of them and would spend many hours developing his battle plans. Unfortunately, these same Army men would often be left in the hallways and other inconvenient places. Accidentally stepping on them in bare feet was not a pleasant experience. As his Army men began to take over the house, tensions developed. This all culminated in his soldiers being collected with a shovel from the garage. Their final fate remains a mystery to this day. However, Santa has been known to put some in his stocking to this day as a friendly reminder.

And the Navy Moves On
Joyce Larson – Bill's sister

As a Navy family, you can expect to move every two to three years. One of our moves involved driving across country to get to our new duty station in San Diego, California. It was the summer of 1958.

We settled in, and right after Christmas we went to visit family friends in Burbank. Our ultimate goal was to see the Rose Bowl Parade in Pasadena on New Year's Day. My Dad was given the task of spending the night on the parade route to ensure that the family would have a great viewing spot for the parade. This was quite an impressionable task for me, as an eight year old to see. I remember watching him leave for his time on the street and hoping he would be okay.

While we were living in California, our Dad spent a lot of time. at sea on aircraft carriers. He was usually gone six months at a stretch Needless to say, Mom had full responsibility for the family. With three young children at that time, she ran a "tight ship".

On one of our Dad's sea duty expeditions, he returned with something he did not have when he left - a mustache!! Mom was not happy at all. She sent him right back onto the ship and told him to shave it off. He was not coming home with us until the mustache was gone. With Mom being a Marine in her younger days, he knew not to argue with her. After all, they were married for over 60 years.

Costumes and Other Bill Antics
Nancy Pennington – Bill's sister

Mom made three bears costumes for us for Halloween as kids in RI.
And then....

- Bill (age 5) gets talked into dressing up as a female with long dress, wig & parasol to advertise his sister's and neighbors' "Backyard Shows"

- Costumes continue to play a theme when Bill dresses up as the devil to help motivate his running trainees get through the "hell" of accomplishing the Boston marathon. Sometimes he is "The devil with the blue dress on"!

- Brings tulip bulbs to his children's elementary school when he read a book about tulips to their class.

- As a teenager, there was a cabbage throwing incident (he was annoyed about something) in his backyard garden.

- Great way to make cole slaw!! And ... it was a clue about his destiny to pursue natural resources in college.

- The Boston Celtics - "Havlicek stole the ball! It's all over!!!" a record album that was played over and over and over! Drove us and our cousin's wife, Laura, (who was a house guest for a month) crazy!!

Bill's Not Gandhi, But They Read From the Same Script
James Greeley

"In order to find yourself, you should lose yourself in the service of others". ~ *Gandhi*

Bill Pennington may have taken this advice as a young Dad when he became involved with the South School PTO. He wanted the best possible educational experience, not just for his kids, but for all the students. He soon became PTO President and his unorthodox methods likely guaranteed, then Principal Dr. Eileen Woods, a spot in the "Patience Hall of Fame". However his passion, enthusiasm, and genuine desire to make South School even better than it already was earned the respect and admiration of all and in 2017 he was one of eight people to be honored as the Andover Rotary "Citizens Who Care Award".

Bill has run and finished 52 Marathons with a personal best time of 2:38:00. However, he had a desire not just to compete, but to help other runners. So he became a coach of Charity Runners. These individuals were not veteran runners but, in most instances, individuals attempting to run their first and, in many cases, only marathon for a designated non-profit. Bill's disciplined training regimen earned him the affectionate nickname of "The Devil". At least I think affectionate. His tough love methods with these novice runners have resulted in hundreds of them finishing the marathon, raising substantial donations for multiple charities, completing a bucket list item and becoming lifelong friends with " The Devil".

Bill's greatest passion in the service of others is his work with the Veterans. Eight years ago he decided to do something for Post 9/11 Veterans. Bill's Mom was a Marine and his Dad a 30-year Navy veteran, so he decided to recognize and honor the men and women who dedicate their lives in the defense of our Country. Managing a race was second nature to a man who in 1992 created the, now legendary, Feaster Five Thanksgiving Race. However, Bill wanted more than a 5K to truly honor these heroes, many who came home severely physically handicapped and psychologically scarred with PTSD. So he added a dinner with an auction and entertainment in order to make the most money possible for the beneficiaries, Homes For Our Troops; Homeland Heroes and Ironstone Farm, in coordination with Home Base Foundation and Mass General who runs 24 weekend retreats each year for Vets with PTSD.

Bill's accomplishments have earned him several richly deserved honors, including The Andover Chamber of Commerce Person of the Year Award, and the Challenge Unlimited Spirit of Giving Award. However, Bill doesn't do it for the accolades. He does it because he actually believes a few caring people can change the world!

I'm just glad Bill still hasn't totally found himself!!

Jim Greeley
Ironstone Farm

Who the **** Is This Guy?
Danny Dwyer

The first time I met Bill was in 2017, the first year I was training to run Boston. I was out at a 5k race for the Fisher House in Mansfield, MA and they had a pancake breakfast after the race. Not sure how we started talking, but once he learned I was running for the Lazarus House, he invited me to sit at his table for breakfast. He then proceeded to introduce me to everyone at the table and everyone at the race he knew. As an introvert I was taken back and remember thinking "Who the fuck is this guy?" I soon would learn that underneath his no BS, no breaking style, lives a man with a heart of gold, one I am grateful to call my friend.

Taxi Ride
By Ben Kellman

I arrived at the address and honked the horn. After waiting a few minutes I honked again. Since this was going to be the last ride of my shift I thought about just driving away, but instead I put the car in park, walked up to the door and knocked. 'Just a minute', answered a frail, elderly voice. I could hear something being dragged across the floor.

After a long pause, the door opened. A small woman in her 90's stood before me. She was wearing a print dress and a pillbox hat with a veil pinned on it, like somebody out of a 1940's movie.

By her side was a small nylon suitcase. The apartment looked as if no one had lived in it for years. All the furniture was covered with sheets.

There were no clocks on the walls, no knickknacks or utensils on the counters. In the corner was a cardboard box filled with photos and glassware.

'Would you carry my bag out to the car?' she said. I took the suitcase to the cab, then returned to assist the woman.

She took my arm and we walked slowly toward the curb.

She kept thanking me for my kindness. 'It's nothing', I told her. 'I just try to treat my passengers the way I would want my mother to be treated.'

'Oh, you're such a good boy, she said. When we got in the cab, she gave me an address and then asked, 'Could you drive through downtown?'

'It's not the shortest way,' I answered quickly.

'Oh, I don't mind,' she said. 'I'm in no hurry. I'm on my way to a hospice.

I looked in the rear-view mirror. Her eyes were glistening. 'I don't have any family left,' she continued in a soft voice. 'The doctor says I don't have very long.' I quietly reached over and shut off the meter.

'What route would you like me to take?' I asked.

For the next two hours, we drove through the city. She showed me the building where she had once worked as an elevator operator.

We drove through the neighborhood where she and her husband had lived when they were newlyweds, She had me pull up in front of a furniture warehouse that had once been a ballroom where she had gone dancing as a girl.

Sometimes she'd ask me to slow in front of a particular building or corner and would sit staring into the darkness, saying nothing.

As the first hint of sun was creasing the horizon, she suddenly said, 'I'm tired. Let's go now'.

We drove in silence to the address she had given me. It was a low building, like a small convalescent home, with a driveway that passed under a portico.

Two orderlies came out to the cab as soon as we pulled up. They were solicitous and intent, watching her every move.

They must have been expecting her.

I opened the trunk and took the small suitcase to the door. The woman was already seated in a wheelchair.

'How much do I owe you?' She asked, reaching into her purse.

'Nothing,' I said

'You have to make a living,' she answered.

'There are other passengers,' I responded.

Almost without thinking, I bent and gave her a hug. She held onto me tightly.

'You gave an old woman a little moment of joy,' she said. 'Thank you.'

I squeezed her hand, and then walked into the dim morning light. Behind me, a door shut. It was the sound of the closing of a life.

I didn't pick up any more passengers that shift. I drove aimlessly lost in thought. For the rest of that day, I could hardly talk. What if that woman had gotten an angry driver, or one who was impatient to end his shift? What if I had refused to take the run, or had honked once, then driven away?

On a quick review, I don't think that I have done anything more important in my life.

We're conditioned to think that our lives revolve around great moments.

But great moments often catch us unaware-beautifully wrapped in what others may consider a small one.

PEOPLE MAY NOT REMEMBER EXACTLY WHAT YOU DID, OR WHAT YOU SAID ~BUT~THEY WILL ALWAYS REMEMBER HOW YOU MADE THEM FEEL.

At the bottom of this great story was a request to forward this - I deleted that request because if you have read to this point, you won't have to be asked to pass it along you just will... Thank you, my friend...

Life may not be the party we hoped for, but while we are here, we might as well dance.

Final Thoughts From Bill

When you look back on your life and realize all the blessings, it helps you get through this really difficult time. Concentrate on the positive.

I'm blessed with memories. It has been a good ride overall. I try to maintain the positive. The coronavirus affects so many and makes life difficult for so many. Telling these stories are among the ways that have helped me get through it. It has been great therapy.

With love and respect, Bill

Made in the USA
Middletown, DE
29 April 2022

64962579R00095